MW01075816

THE PRACTICE OF *A COURSE IN MIRACLES*

FORM versus CONTENT:

SEX and MONEY

KENNETH WAPNICK, Ph.D.

Foundation for A COURSE IN MIRACLES®

Foundation for A Course in Miracles®
41397 Buecking Drive
Temecula, CA 92590
www.facim.org

First printing, 2005

Printed in the United States of America

Portions of *A Course in Miracles* copyright 1992
Psychotherapy: Purpose, Process and Practice copyright 1976, 1992
The Song of Prayer copyright 1976, 1992
by the *Foundation for A Course in Miracles*®

Library of Congress Cataloging-in-Publication Data

Wapnick, Kenneth, 1942-
  Form vs. content : sex and money / Kenneth Wapnick.
    p. cm.
  Includes index.
  ISBN 13: 978-1-59142-194-8
  ISBN 10: 1-59142-194-2
  1. Course in miracles. 2. Sex--Miscellanea. 3. Money--Miscellanea. I. Title: Form versus content. II. Title.
  BP605.C68W3592 2005
  299'.93--dc22   2005018731

CONTENTS

Preface

This book—*Form versus Content: Sex and Money*
—is an edited transcript of the workshop of the same
name, given at the Foundation in 2002. It is a contin-
uation of a series of classes and publications that address the application of the Course's principles to
specific aspects of our lives. The informal series began several years ago with the publication of a little
book on overeating. Though the focus of these books
may vary, they all reflect the importance of seeing the
activity—hence the problems surrounding it—within
the larger perspective of the ego's strategy to root our
attention in *form*, to the neglect of *content*. This will
be discussed in the Introduction, as well as throughout
the book.

The workshop began with an extensive introduction
that summarized the metaphysical underpinnings of
the theme of *form-content*. An understanding of these
is essential for the proper appreciation of both the ego's
and Jesus' use of sex and money. Since this summary
can be found in different forms in many publications—
audio, video, and books—especially *All Are Called*,
Volume One of *The Message of A Course in Miracles*,
it has been greatly abbreviated to focus only on the
ego's aforementioned strategy. This will lead us into

the discussion of sex and money, two areas that are among the most guilt-laden in the ego's vast repertory of potential objects for its projections.

As with the other books in this series on the practice of *A Course in Miracles*, we have edited the transcript of the original workshop to make it more readable, at the same time seeking to maintain the informality of the workshop. Some additional material has been provided as well, which includes the summarizing statement (found in Chapter 4) drawn from questions asked in a class held the following day on a different topic.

Rosemarie LoSasso, the Foundation's Publication Director, applied her excellent editorial skills, as usual, to the evolution of the manuscript from a raw transcript to one that could be more easily read. I could not be more grateful for her invaluable help.

1. Introduction

Mind and the Split Mind

To speak about *form* and *content* as it applies to our everyday lives, specifically sex and money, we must begin at the Beginning. God is the first and only Content, along with His creation, Christ. God and Christ, Father and Son, are one in Thought, united in Mind. When the impossible appeared to have happened —the tiny, mad idea that the Son could be separate from his Source—a new content arose: separation, in which the Mind of Christ appeared to be split into Mind and mind.

The split mind now splits into a wrong and right mind, home of the ego and Holy Spirit respectively. These represent two mutually exclusive ways of looking at the tiny, mad idea. The ego sees it as reality, while the Holy Spirit does not see it at all, for the separation from God never happened—the principle of the Atonement. Thus the Content of the Mind of God —love—is replaced by the two contents of the split mind: separation and Atonement. A third part of the mind—the decision maker—chooses between them. Enamored of the separation, which ensures its existence as a separate entity, the Son of God—equated

1

with the decision maker—allies itself with the thought of the ego and believes itself to be an autonomous and independent self, no longer part of undifferentiated and undivided Oneness. To invoke one of the Course's principal metaphors, we can say that the Son of God fell asleep and began his dream of separation, yet all the while retaining a memory of his reality as the pre-separated state of spirit—God's one Son as He created him.

The Ego's Strategy—Mindlessness

The ego, fresh from its victory over the Holy Spirit, now finds itself face to face with a mortal enemy—the Son of God himself. Wishing only to maintain the separate self it won, the part of the mind that chose the ego wants to ensure that the mind never changes its decision, for its existence as a special and differentiated self depends on the power of the Son's mind to believe it is self-created rather than God-created. We shall see presently how this power of self-creation becomes an important thought in the areas of sex and money. If that belief is withdrawn, the ego's separate self will disappear back into the nothingness from which it came. Thus the ego perceives the power of the Son's mind to choose as its greatest threat, and must do something to nullify this sword of Damocles hanging over its tenuous head—the power to choose against it and for the Holy Spirit.

Enter now the ego's strategy to devise a plan so the Son of God will never change his mind. Its goal is simple, and its means to achieve it ingenious. Its sole purpose is to make the Son of God mindless, for if he no longer knows he has—and *is*—a mind, he cannot change it. And so the ego adopts the plan to make the mind so abhorrent and terrifying that the Son will voluntarily wish to leave it, thereby becoming mindless, ensuring that the original decision for the ego remains permanent and its existence secured.

The ego's plan centers on instilling the fear of God—literally—in the Son's mind. It tells the Son a story—a cosmic myth—the purpose being to cause the Son to choose to flee his mind, never to return. The foundation block of the ego's story is the unholy trinity of sin, guilt, and fear. Here is the tale, briefly summarized:

We have *sinned* against God. By selfishly wanting our separation, a price had to be paid for our freedom—God had to be destroyed since oneness and separation cannot coexist. Where one is, the other can never be. And since we believe we are separated, this means that God's living Oneness had to be sacrificed. Therefore our individual existence is forever equated

3

with sin, which is woven into the very fabric of our existence—if I exist I must be a sinner, because sin is how I separated.

Guilt, then, is the inevitable consequence, for it tells us not only that we have committed an un-redeemable sin by shattering Heaven's Oneness, destroying our Creator and crucifying His Son, but we are inherently unredeemable because we *are* sinful—our individuality now inextricably interwoven with sin.

Finally, our sin deserves punishment. Since the object of our sin is God, our newly made Enemy now returns from the grave to take back from us the life we believe we stole from Him. And thus we *fear* His Love, believing it will destroy us.

In this way the mind, heretofore the celebratory home of our existence, becomes a battleground of death, which will surely come at the wrathful hands of our God, hell-bent on returning the compliment of seizing life. We now have a serious problem confronting us—instant annihilation. Remember, however, that this problem is non-existent, for there is no angry God, no sin to be punished. This is but the ego's made-up story to motivate us to choose mindlessness. The true problem is that we—the one Son of God—have believed in the ego rather than the Holy Spirit, and having made that choice, *everything* that followed was simply a way of preserving our mistaken decision.

This important point is the foundation of our later discussion of sex and money. This problem of our wrong choice the ego never wants us to acknowledge; otherwise we would certainly change it. Note how cleverly the ego sets up a false problem, beginning with wedding individuality with sin. Thus, its tale of *sin, guilt,* and *fear* is purposive. In the Course, Jesus tells us that when we understand purpose we understand everything, and the only thing we should ask of anything is *what is it for?* (T-17.VI.2:1-2). Therefore, to understand sex and money, we first have to understand the ego's purpose for the world and body: to distract us from its real problem—the mind's decision maker—so we can never again identify with its power to choose against the ego.

The Body: A Maladaptive Solution
to a Non-Existent Problem

Pursuing its strategy, the ego sought to drive us out of our minds—literally and figuratively—to attain its goal of mindlessness. It succeeded in blotting from awareness the Content of God's Love by convincing us to choose against its reflected content, the Holy Spirit's Atonement principle. This left only the ego's content of separation, now identified with sin. By so doing, the clever ego shifted the problem from the decision-making mind to the spurious problem of sin, and its certain consequence of destruction. To "solve" this problem, the ego counseled us to flee the mind—the perceived locus of the problem—and seek refuge in the world and body. Thus was the physical universe "created" through the dynamic of projection, in fear of God's punishment. The ego's made-up problem of sin and guilt—its *content*—now was seen in the world of *form*—the body's life of suffering and pain. Yet it was all made up—*a maladaptive solution to a non-existent problem.* And so our individual self was preserved, as the ego successfully consummated its strategy of making the Son of God mindless, one among billions of fragments of God's Son.

To seal our fate of being separated, the ego caused a veil to fall across our minds, so we have no recollection that we are children of the ego, let alone children of God. Believing now that we are bodies, the content of *both* love and guilt has been buried beneath the form; the Self of love concealed by the decision-making self of guilt, which in turn has been concealed by the body, the embodiment of the ego's thought system of separation. And so we identify as mindless creatures, without being able even to use the word—since *mindless* means we lack a mind, which we no longer even know exists—and think of ourselves only as bodies, governed by a brain, determined by a genetic code, and influenced by our environment.

The world of bodies—collective and personal—directly expresses the wrong-minded thought system of the ego, yet conceals it. Thus does the unholy trinity of sin, guilt, and fear manifest *outside* the mind, though in truth it always remains *within* it, reflecting the principle that *ideas leave not their source*: the content of the mind can never leave its source—the Son's decision—and move to the world of form, our appearance and experience to the contrary. Therefore, regardless of what we believe, the source of our unhappiness and pain does not emanate from the world—forces and agents beyond our control—but the mind's decision for the ego. The mind's battleground of *kill or be killed* has become the content of the world.

It was that thought of *one or the other* that literally gave rise to our separated existence, and continues to sustain it. This explains why our lives are fraught with guilt, fear, and conflict—*ideas leave not their source*—as is the case so very frequently with sex and money. We can see how the body—physically and psychologically—was specifically made in the image and likeness of the ego's underlying content. Consider again what the ego has done in developing its myth. Its story of sin, guilt, and fear substitutes a non-existent problem for the ego's real problem of the mind's power to choose against it. And so the ego made a problem to conceal the true problem, and then projected *its* problem to form a multiplicity of non-existent problems. All these involve the body, and embrace concerns with oxygen, water, food, shelter, loneliness, sickness, and death. Sex becomes a necessity to ensure the survival of the species, and secondarily to meet hormonal and emotional needs, while earning money is essential for individual survival. Since *ideas leave not their source*, the world's problems shadow the mind's problem of the non-existent battleground of *one or the other*, *kill or be killed*. How very far that takes us, then, from the decision-making mind that is the problem and the answer!

Clearly, there is no way we could survive as physical/psychological creatures unless we solved our basic problems of need satisfaction. For example, an infant learns very early on how to solve the problem of hunger or thirst. It cries, getting its parents' attention. Soon after, when it craves attention, seeks comfort, or wants to be held, it either throws a tantrum or smiles sweetly. In this fashion, we begin our lives in the body by quickly learning to solve the problems of life and getting our needs met. Thus it is that everything in the world is an attempt to solve a problem. And again, all our problems center on the body—the ego's maladaptive solution to the non-existent problem of remaining in the mind. The ego has brilliantly made up a problem that necessitates a solution, which in turn becomes a problem that necessitates a solution, which becomes a problem, and on and on and on. No sooner do we solve one problem than another rises to take its place, as is cogently expressed in two parallel workbook Lessons, 79 and 80: "Let me recognize my problem so it can be solved" and "Let me recognize that all my problems have been solved." Obviously, nothing truly gets resolved because *there is nothing there to resolve.*

Looking at the body objectively, one can easily see the ego's strategy of setting up perpetual problems for perpetual dis-ease*; e.g., perhaps we solve the problems of food, money, or health today, but what about the future? I may finally have learned to satisfy my needs, but that does not mean the same plan will work tomorrow, next week, or next year. Our attention—both as individuals and members of society—is thus continually focused on non-existent problems demanding maladaptive solutions, for the world of form (the body) was specifically made to defend against the world of content (the mind)—the state of mindlessness the ego sees as salvation.

---

* This phrase is borrowed from historian Charles Beard's description of American foreign policy since World War II of waging *perpetual war for perpetual peace.*

The Correction

Yet the Holy Spirit's reason tells us that

> the form of error is not what makes it a mistake. If what the form conceals is a mistake, the form cannot prevent correction (T-22.III.5:1-2).

The problem is not the *form*, but the uses we have made of it: the *content*—which means the purpose of erecting a physical smoke screen so we would never see the real problem, which is the part of our minds that chose the ego instead of the Holy Spirit. No two areas are better suited than sex and money for this specific purpose of wedding us to form so that we would not look at content, as we shall see presently. The following passage from "Reason and the Forms of Error" nicely summarizes the ego's purpose for the body—to see the world of *form* and conceal the mind's *content*:

> The body's eyes see only form. They cannot see beyond what they were made to see. And they were made to look on error and not see past it. Theirs is indeed a strange perception, for they can see only illusions, unable to look beyond the granite block of sin, and stopping at the outside form of nothing. To this distorted form of vision the outside of everything, the wall that stands between you and the truth, is wholly true. Yet how can sight that

stops at nothingness, as if it were a solid wall, see
truly? It is held back by form, having been made
to guarantee that nothing else but form will be
perceived.

These eyes, made not to see, will never see. For
the idea they represent [the reality of the sin of
separation] left not its maker [the decision
maker], and it is their maker that sees through
them. What was its maker's goal but not to see?
For this the body's eyes are perfect means, but not
for seeing. See how the body's eyes rest on externals and cannot go beyond. Watch how they
stop at nothingness, unable to go beyond the form
to meaning. Nothing so blinding as perception of
form. For sight of form means understanding has
been obscured (T-22.III.5:3–6:8).

This is but one among dozens of passages throughout *A Course in Miracles* that explain how the body
was made to see without seeing, hear without hearing,
think without thinking. Therefore, eyes do not see,
ears do not hear, brains do not think, for they were
made to perceive only what the ego told them to perceive, and to think only what they were programmed
to think—separation, sin, and guilt; in other words, to
look on the error of form and not see past it to the
mind.

Thus was the body made to suffer—the ego's
maladaptive solution—physically and psychologically, and to experience conflict regarding the things

of the world; e.g., sex and money. The ego's principle here is that the more guilt inducing and fearful the form, the less likely we are to move to the mind, where the Holy Spirit exposes the world's purpose of being the source of guilt and fear. We want our eyes always to focus on the body—ours and other people's —and never on the mind. The ego knows that there remains a part of the mind that knows the body is nothing. Like in the fairy tale, our right mind recognizes that the ego's emperor—ruling the kingdom of sin, guilt, and fear—is made up. Moreover, not only does the emperor have no clothes, *there is no emperor*. Yet the nothingness is given reality by our fearful need to escape from it and make a world to escape from a problem that does not exist, and then make bodily problems to complete the defensive shield against the mind's decision-making power.

As we have already discussed, this is a brilliantly conceived strategy, and most successful because very few throughout history have penetrated the ego's defensive shield of the world and body. We still believe there is something out there to be overcome, problems that have to be confronted. However, the only problem to be solved is the mistake of believing there is a world and body that are the cause of pain and suffering. We know that perception lies because it stops at the form and does not go beyond it to the mind. We have seen that the body's sensory apparatus was specifically made to rest only on externals, which is why we should never trust what they report: "Nothing so blinding as perception of form." We need to recognize that everything here is perception of form because, again, the body was made to conceal the mind's content of guilt, which itself was made to conceal the true content of the mind's power to choose.

Within the dream, our only self-concept is that of decision maker—the power to choose the ego or the Holy Spirit. Consequently, the Holy Spirit's reason—right-minded thinking—has another purpose for the body, which is to be a classroom in which we learn the difference between form and content, illusion and truth. Returning to "Reason and the Forms of Error," we read:

> Reason will tell you that if form is not reality it must be an illusion, and is not there to see. And if you see it you must be mistaken, for you are seeing what can *not* be real as if it were. What cannot see beyond what is not there must be distorted perception, and must perceive illusions as the truth. Could it, then, recognize the truth? (T-22.III.7:4-7)

The content of *A Course in Miracles* is the right-minded thought system of the Holy Spirit's reason—forgiveness—which corrects the ego's mistaken thought system of guilt and hate. Whatever the ego made to reinforce belief in the illusion of its own existence, Jesus uses as the means of undoing it. This will be the focus of our discussion of sex and money. Once the world of bodies was made to serve the unholy purpose of keeping the memory of God away from our decision maker, the world became neutral, capable of serving the ego's wrong-minded purpose of keeping us asleep, or the Holy Spirit's right-minded purpose of awakening us. This means that our bodies can now become behavioral expressions of the mind's underlying thought system: expressing hate or love, conflict or joining.

Reason, or vision, means that we look at the world from above the battleground—i.e., the mind—the only sane way to look at anything in the world. This means we return to the decision-making part of the mind. When we do so, we must be with Jesus because the ego would never lead us there. At this point the decision maker becomes an observer, looking at the body's activities and understanding they but reflect the mind's content—looking from the perspective of the dreamer, not the dream. We thus no longer identify with the dream figure—the person we call ourselves and recognize each morning in the mirror—but the dreamer who made the dream to serve the purpose of its teacher.

And so we look at the ego without guilt, fear, or judgment, for we look through the Holy Spirit's eyes and with Jesus' love beside us, realizing the body's world is but a dream. As we increasingly understand Jesus' teachings, we recognize that everything we experience within the linear world of time and space is a shadowy fragment of the thought system of sin, guilt, and fear. Therefore, we can choose again: God over the ego, Atonement over separation, content over form.

Introduction to Sex and Money

I preface my discussion of sex and money by telling two stories. Both have to do with psychotherapy, but their content can generalize to our topic and thus provide a good introduction.

I joined Helen Schucman and William Thetford in the late spring of 1973,* and after completing my second reading of *A Course in Miracles* in the fall, I asked Helen if she had scribed anything else. She mentioned that there was something on psychotherapy that was obviously not finished, but I was welcome to look at it. Coming from a background in psychotherapy, I was obviously interested in seeing it. What Helen showed me was complete at that point through the first six sections in Chapter 2 of what would become the pamphlet, *Psychotherapy: Purpose, Process and Practice*. After reading the material, I rather disappointedly told Helen that this was exactly like the Course. I no longer remember her response, though I suspect she probably said to me, in effect, somewhat incredulously: "What else did you think it would be?" Clearly, I had expected this material on psychotherapy would be different, a

_____

* My book *Absence from Felicity* chronicles the details of my relationship with Helen Schucman, scribe of the Course and her associate and friend William Thetford.

kind of how-to book, replete with examples, case studies, etc. Readers familiar with the pamphlet know that it is, naturally, just like *A Course in Miracles*, insofar as it applies the principles of healing—two people coming together to share a common interest—to psychotherapy.

The second story relates to a week-long workshop I gave at a retreat center in Idaho in the mid-1980s. A psychiatrist was among those attending, and early in the week he asked if I could devote some time to talking about *A Course in Miracles* and psychotherapy, as he had read the pamphlet and was interested in hearing more about it. I said that if there were time later in the week I would do so, which I did near the end of the class. When I finished, he raised his hand and said, echoing my "complaint" to Helen: "You didn't say anything different from what you have been saying all week."

I therefore want to warn readers that they will not find what I have to say about sex and money any different from what I have said in the Introduction—or for that matter, in any of my work. The point of those two stories, which in a sense is the basis for this discussion of sex and money, is that problems pertaining to them, or to any other specific problem area, are all the same. Whatever our problems around sex and money—variations of special love or special hate—they do not differ from any other issue in our lives. I could certainly have added food, since for many people this is a major symbol and goes to the ontological heart of the ego's thought system, as indeed do sex and money. I did not include it, however, because in general food tends not to be an interpersonal phenomenon.* However, as an example of how the same principles apply to food issues, I have included in the Appendix a brief dialogue I had with a student during a recent class. Finally, I will keep the topics of sex and money separate, but there is obviously an overlap when we consider their ontological antecedents and underlying ego purpose.

---

* Several years ago I had a discussion with three Course students on the topic of food and weight issues. The discussion was recorded and is available on a single tape (#T-26 "Overeating: A Dialogue"), and also in book form (#B-12). See Related Material at the end of the book for further information.

2. Sex

Introduction

This presentation on sex has a history, traced back to the first time I gave a workshop with sex as one of the topics. It was in the early 1980s in Seattle. Before going there, my wife Gloria and I stopped off in the Bay Area to visit Judy Skutch and Bill Thetford. Judy had just received a copy of *The Spiritual Sex Manual*, claimed to be channeled from Jesus. Gloria suggested I look at the book since the author was from the Seattle area, and she correctly thought that people at the workshop would be asking about it. I did look through it, and to say something positive about the book before pointing out a drawback, it can serve a helpful purpose, as one of its goals is to teach its readers not to be guilty over sex. What makes the book unusual, however, is that it is quite explicit in describing how one has sex with Jesus. In one scene in the book, in fact, the authoress is making love to her husband, whose place is suddenly taken by Jesus who consummates the act, with quite explicit and specific details about the love-making. In its emphasis on form, I think the book got off track, although the content of not feeling guilty about sex is, again, helpful.

2. SEX

I do not usually comment on other spiritual writings, but I bring up *The Spiritual Sex Manual* because it sets the stage for our discussion of sex. The error found in that book—from the perspective of *A Course in Miracles*—is that it focuses quite heavily on behavior—*form,* not *content.* Therefore, in discussing the emotionally laden subject of sex, it is essential that its underlying context be understood, without which the ego's purpose of separation and defense will ultimately prevail. Incidentally, I did spend part of the workshop in Seattle talking about sex, and have done so from time to time since then, as well as in some of my books.*

The Importance of Sex in the Ego Thought System

I begin with a passage from the text. I am taking it out of context, but its content is what I wish to call your attention to. It is from the section called "Atonement without Sacrifice" (T-3.I), which contains Jesus' critique of the Christian view of Atonement: God's

---

* See for example, "The Meaning of Love and Sexuality," Chapter 4 in my *Forgiveness and Jesus: The Meeting Place of A COURSE IN MIRACLES and Christianity.* See also the Electronic Outreach on our Web site (www.facim.org): Question & Answer Service – Index of Topics: Money; Relationships / sexuality.

plan of sacrifice to save us from our sinfulness. In the second paragraph, Jesus states that at the core of Christian theology is the "terrible misperception that God Himself persecuted His Own Son on behalf of salvation" (T-3.I.2:4). Then he says, and this is the relevant part:

> The very words are meaningless. It has been particularly difficult to overcome this [the misperception that God caused Jesus to suffer for us] because, although the error itself is no harder to correct than any other, many have been unwilling to give it up in view of its prominent value as a defense (T-3.I.2:5-6).

The area of sex, and money as well, is a difficult issue because, among other things, it almost always leads students in spiritual disciplines, including *A Course in Miracles*, to misinterpret the paths they are following. The reason for this is *its prominent value as a defense*, which leads to the confusion of form and content.

From a biological perspective, sex is the way we reproduce and thereby preserve our species—the way we create life. It is a biological fact that we come into existence as a result of a union of sperm and egg, representing the original separation from God that began the instant the ego believed it was on its own, directing the course of its own life. At that instant we became self-created rather than God-created. The body is thus nothing more or less than the expression in form of this underlying thought that we can create life that is independent of our Creator and Source—the heart of the separation fallacy. In "The Laws of Chaos," Jesus says:

> There is no life outside of Heaven. Where God created life, there life must be. In any state apart from Heaven life is illusion (T-23.II.19:1-3).

We therefore believe we usurped God's place on the throne of creation, and within the ego thought system have the illusion of being creators, essentially negating the biblical story of creation. The projection of this unconscious thought system results in a world of bodies, which then become the instruments of self-creation. And here is where the problem lies, explaining why sex, certainly in our society, has almost always been a major problem—fraught with guilt, anxiety, fear, and certainly specialness. Recall the Introduction—the original thought that we are on our own and can indeed create life is equated by the ego with *sin*, leading to *guilt*, and then *fear* of punishment. On the most basic level, then, being in a body symbolizes guilt. For example, taking a breath is the way we keep our bodies alive, and can be construed as a way of saying to God: "The breath of your spirit is not enough for me. I need something outside You to sustain my life because

You will not give me what I want." Our need for food and water makes the same statement, as do our emotional needs, and so we continually thumb our nose in God's face and tell Him we do not need Him, since He has already made it clear that He does not recognize our existence.

When looked at within this ontological context, sex likewise tells God that not only do we not need Him, but we can do everything He can. The height of our arrogance is the belief that we can do things better than He. The true God, for example, cannot kill, while we are quite adept in that area. Thus, not only can we create life, but we can destroy it too. When we, as one Son, made the cosmos, we made an incredibly vast, and to us at least, a most impressive world. We never cease to be awestruck by what we have done. On a beautifully clear, star-filled night we look up and are overwhelmed, finding great inspiration in the vastness of the sky. We marvel at the beauty of a sunrise or sunset. Yet in back of all this we say to our Creator: "You see, I can make a world every bit as grand as Yours." And on the microcosmic level of our dream, through sex, we do indeed create life. When sex is understood from this perspective, we see that the many problems surrounding it have nothing to do with sexual *behavior*, but rather with the *underlying thought of guilt* that says: "I am a god who has destroyed God,

25

taking His creative life for my own." Sex becomes but another way of reminding ourselves that we have sinfully usurped God's function and supplanted Him.

In the manual for teachers there is a powerful account of the original error (M-17), one of many places in *A Course in Miracles* that clearly enunciate the sin-guilt-fear trinity. Jesus describes our fear of God catching up with us, and how we bury in our minds what we believe we did to Him and what He will do in retaliation. But then comes this horrifying thought: "Think not He has forgotten" (M-17.7:4). In other words, do not for one minute think that God has forgotten what you did; and so do not think that He will not pursue you and exact His deadly vengeance. If sex is one of the prominent ways in which we demonstrate our divinity through "creating" life, imagine the unconscious guilt and terror associated with this sin-filled reminder.

Think, too, about the fact that when the ego made its sexual scenario, it also made it pleasurable. From an evolutionary point of view this makes perfect sense, as there would need to be a way to induce members of a species to copulate so the species would be preserved. As we can see in homo sapiens, however, the behavior has become divorced from its original purpose, and so now sex is most frequently pursued solely for pleasure, an added burden of guilt, for now pleasure is derived from the act that ultimately symbolizes the death of

God—we not only succeeded in usurping our Creator's role, but now enjoy it! It is this guilt that manifests in the various issues and problems that have arisen surrounding sex: birth control, abortion, sexual orientation, pre- and extra-marital sex, sexual dysfunction, etc.

As we are able to join Jesus in viewing sex from his perspective above the battleground, outside the dream, we see that everything experienced within the linear world of time and space is a shadowy fragment of that one original thought. How could sex *not* have turned into such a negative symbol of the special relationship—special love or special hate, where the relationship becomes the source of suffering, hurt, and loss (special hate), or pleasure, contentment, and completion (special love).

Let me say before I go much further that in no way does any of this mean that we should feel guilty because we enjoy sex or because it is an important part of our life, any more than we should feel guilty because we like what money can do for us. Recall this important dimension of the Course's teaching: once the world was made for an unholy purpose—which includes sex and money—it becomes neutral. Made to keep us in the dream of separation through guilt and specialness, the world can continue to serve that purpose, or be the means of our learning forgiveness and awakening from the dream. Later we shall read from

27

"The Special Function," an important discussion of how the Holy Spirit uses for healing what the ego made for harm.

Returning to the ontological perspective of sex, it can be readily understood why it became such a prominent symbol. Instead of being just one biological function among others, it is now a *prominent* biological function. It has become tempting for many people to spiritualize sex, making it into something holy. Yet nothing of the body could be holy—or *un*holy—for it is neutral. Again, bodily activity can serve the holy purpose of forgiveness, or the unholy purpose of reinforcing specialness. To reiterate this point, of itself the body is nothing, and so having sex is not a spiritual *or* profane activity. Its value depends solely on the purpose it serves.

It is therefore crucial to understand the ontological roots of sex, for it will explain why it is such a burning issue in our world. I remember a history professor from my college days—a delightful British gentleman with a different way of expressing things from almost everyone else in the department—who said that the world's history is written in the bedroom: if you want to learn how and why things happened throughout history, study what went on in the bedchambers of kings and rulers.

The section on "The Obstacles to Peace" in the text refers to our attraction to guilt, pain, and death, all of which can be subsumed under the more general category of attraction to the body (T-19.IV). We want the body to be real, and it does not matter whether it is in excruciating pain or the ecstasy of sensual pleasure. Sex clearly makes the body real, whether as a way of producing children, having a good time, or a combination of both; whether sex is guilt inducing, or a source of repeated pleasure. The body remains the central focus, and that focus is the real attraction. This holds for almost any other bodily activity as well, but sex is an especially useful defense, a most effective way of dealing with form instead of content. That does not make sex any more or less meaningful than any other physical or psychological activity, but it helps explain our fixation with it. It is almost never regarded as a normal human activity, which would virtually put the entertainment and fashion industries out of business. Madison Avenue cannot even sell toothpaste or cars without sexual innuendos or subliminal sexual messages.

One of the reasons Freud was so attached to his sexual theory was its link to biology. Sex was more to him than genital activity. He spoke of infantile stages of sexuality, and in general defined sex as the basis of human energy. Freud began his career as a neurologist and physician, and at the end of his life predicted that his theories of the mind (sic) would one day be explained electrochemically. I am oversimplifying his position, but this electrochemical connection was extremely important to him because it rooted sex in the body. His fervent defense of psychoanalytic theory reflected the importance of establishing its basic tenets in the physical. As in so many other areas, the father of psychoanalysis was on to something important, but not for the reasons he thought. Sex confirms the reality of the body, and it cannot be stressed enough that the ego made the world and body so we would be distracted, ensuring we would never return to the mind. The result is our constant focus on form at the expense of content.

From the point of view of the special relationship, sex holds such a central place in the ego thought system because it is not something you can do with everyone—by its very bodily expression it can be performed with relatively few, and inevitably demands exclusivity—despite the best efforts of some people! Early in Mozart's great opera, *Don Giovanni* (Don Juan), the hero has jilted still another of his lovers, Donna Elvira, who is crushed because she naively believed Don Giovanni loved her. In an attempt at consolation, the Don's valet, Leporello, a funny fellow indeed, sings his famous Catalog Aria (*Madamina, il catalogo e questo*) to her. He whips out his "not little book" (*questo non piciol libro*), in which are recorded all his master's conquests, including 640

Italians, 231 Germans, 100 French, 91 Turks, and in Spain "already 1,003" (*son gia mille e tre*)! Not surprisingly, psychologists speak of the "Don Juan complex," where a man wants to have as many women as possible, reflecting the ultimate fantasy of conquering the world and thereby becoming God.

The complex notwithstanding, sex is clearly something that occurs between separate people, as opposed to the *thought of love* that embraces God's Sons as one. Sex is exclusive by definition—you have sex with one person, or in some cases even with more than one person at a time; but it cannot be everyone, clearly reflecting the fundamental ego thought system of separation and exclusivity. Sex is *one or the other*, what the ego said at the beginning to God: "I am going to get my pleasure at Your expense." Anything in the world that reinforces separation, exclusivity, and specialness— different words for the same phenomenon—fits in perfectly with the ego's strategy of making a mindless body that seems to keep us separate from each other: "Thus were specifics [i.e., bodies] made" (W-pI.161.3:1).

Jesus says in the text: "Minds are joined; bodies are not" (T-18.VI.3:1). The *thought of love* in the mind joins everyone as one. On the other hand, the *expression of love* in the body is limited, and in that sense sex is a limited activity, and thus a symbol for the ego's limitation, as is the body itself (T-18.VIII.1:1-4). This does not make it either good or bad, simply a perceptual fact that shadows for us the underlying thought of the ego that says separation is real. Again, this explains the attraction to sex—both as a problem to be solved and as something we value. Yet it can serve a different purpose, to which we shall return. However, the primary reason it is such a problem area is its value as a defense, which protects us from ever getting back to our minds.

Remember that the fundamental problem for the ego is the threat inherent in the power of the Son's mind to choose. The ego fears the decision maker, but as part of its survival strategy it declares that this is not the problem, which, instead, is sin, guilt, and fear. Therefore, the problem is no longer that we *chose* to separate, but that we *are* separate, a state the ego equates with sin. By making the wrong-minded thought system real and a constant preoccupation, the ego has blotted from awareness our true self-concept as decision maker. The imaginary problem of the mind's sin, guilt, and fear prevents us from returning to the only problem—the decision maker's mistaken choice for the ego. Having replaced the real problem with this illusory and horrifying one, the ego says the only conceivable solution is to deny the "problem" altogether, project it in the magical hope—though the ego omits the adjective *magical*—we will be forever free of it, for it is now in the world. Thus the body—burdened with innumerable and unending needs and concerns.

The body, then, is the ego's solution to its made-up problem of sin, guilt, and fear in the Son's mind. Yet it is a solution that engenders a host of other problems —physical and psychological—which we spend the rest of our lives trying to solve, oblivious to the fact they were specifically made so as not to be solved. Our attention is thus taken further and further from the decision maker, the unconscious part of our self that wants to be a separated, autonomous individual, but does not want to be punished for its sin. That part yearns for problems, because the more we have, the less likely we are to return to the problem's source in the mind where it would surely be undone. These problems clearly include the sexual, and so we have the sexual problems, issues, and concerns that burden us as individuals and as a society. What helps us deal with these concerns is separating *form* from *content*, facilitated by focusing on *purpose*. This enables us to discover the true nature of the problem, and most importantly, that it is made up. We therefore learn that we *want* to have a bodily problem, preoccupation, or concern—anything that will command our attention, a wonderfully effective means of keeping us mindless —the method in the ego's madness.

2. SEX

We can see, then, how sex is extremely valuable in the ego's hierarchy of defenses. Everyone has a body, part and parcel of which is sexuality, along with its many and varied problems and issues. Society, for example, determines what sexual behavior is normal and what is deviant. From a sociological or anthropological point of view, we can observe how customs and values change. These have nothing to do with any inherent biological phenomenon, because there is no inherent biological phenomenon. Our preferences—whether involving sex, food, or anything else—do not have their source in the body. And even though we are becoming more adept at seeing connections between genetic make-up and addictions, food issues, allergies, and sexual impulses, the fact remains that genes are not the cause of our problems and needs:

> Appetites are "getting" mechanisms, representing the ego's need to confirm itself. This is as true of body appetites as it is of the so-called "higher ego needs." *Body appetites are not physical in origin* (T-4.II.7:5-7; italics mine).

The body is thus a cosmic plot of the ego—the part of the mind that wants to remain separated—to distract us from the only real threat to our existence: the power of the mind to choose.

Sex is high on our list of problems, but it is helpful to realize that the dynamic that made sex a problem is independent of the body, having nothing to do with what sex researchers may tell us, but rather with the underlying purpose that is common to everyone. This is why the first and foremost principle of miracles is that there is no order of difficulty among them (T-1.I.1:1). Every problem is the same, regardless of its form. Recall the important line in the text: "Nothing so blinding as perception of form" (T-22.III.6:7). Form means body, as does sex. And *body* includes not only the physical, but the psychological self as well.

The most healing way of working with sexual issues, then, is ultimately to divorce them from their behavioral expression—not in terms of the act of sex, but in *thinking* about them—seeing them within the larger context from above the battleground, where we recognize they are no different from anything else. The *Psychotherapy* pamphlet explains, in the context of physical sickness, that the form of the symptoms can reveal the form of unforgiveness in the mind, but Jesus quickly points out that this insight into the form of unforgiveness is not necessarily going to help you. Only *forgiveness* heals:

> … a careful study of the form a sickness takes will point quite clearly to the form of unforgiveness that it represents. Yet seeing this will not effect a cure. That is achieved by only one recognition;

that only forgiveness heals an unforgiveness....
(P-2.VI.5:3-5).

In other words, we need not know the specific connection between a symptom and the underlying ego
thought, because in the end all we need do is forgive.
This means not giving the external any power over us.
With this realization the problem disappears, regardless of its form. If we analyzed any sexual symptom,
therefore, we would find it expressed an underlying
thought—some aspect of the ego's belief in separation
and specialness. For example, frigidity in both sexes—
fear of penetration or impotence—can be traced back
to past abuses, fantasies of attack or castration; yet the
bottom line remains the fear of punishment for our sin
of separation. And so the inability to perform sexually
could ultimately be understood as the need to withhold
love as means of protecting the self. Or in experiences
of jealousy, we can easily see the projection of the belief that love has been won through thievery and de-
ception, setting up the inevitable punishment of having
the same fate befall us. As the text explains:

> ...those who project are vigilant for their own
> safety. They are afraid that their projections will
> return and hurt them. Believing they have blotted
> their projections from their own minds, they also
> believe their projections are trying to creep back
> in (T-7.VIII.3:9-11).

The benefit of an exercise like the above, whether seeking to understand a sexual issue, physical symptom, or any other problem, is that it puts into context our little life—and all lives are little. We realize that the bodily life we have, along with everyone else's—past, present, and future—is a fragment of the one life we share as God's insane Son. We differ only in the ways in which we express this insanity, which has but one root cause: the mind's decision to believe the ego instead of the Holy Spirit. There is, again, no order of difficulty in miracles because the *miracle* is the Course's name for the process of bringing the mind's identification with the dream figure—regardless of the dream's forms—back to the dreamer: "The miracle establishes you dream a dream, and that its content is not true" (T-28.II.7:1). The solution to any and all problems is the same: we bring them from their expression as form to their one ego content; thousands upon thousands of different forms, but the content of guilt is one. This content shifts by our no longer judging the guilt as sinful, but forgiving it as simply a mistake. This shift in healing is the same as is expressed in *Psychotherapy*, wherein the therapist sets aside his judgments and belief that he is separate from his patient (P-3.II.6:1; 7:1-2).

We thus recognize that regardless of the form of a problem, its healing is the same. Even though sexual issues are different from other forms of human experience, the source of the anxieties, concerns, and specialness invested in them is the same. Content is understood through understanding purpose, and the ego's purpose for sex is to keep us identified with the body so we are blinded to the mind. As long we remain mindless bodies, we can never change the mind. Everything comes back to that basic idea, which is why I keep repeating it.

One of Freud's most significant contributions was his understanding that dreams are the fulfillment of wishes. Jesus would take that same idea and expand it to include *all* of our dreams—sleeping and waking. They fulfill the decision maker's wish to keep its separate identity as an individual entity, but not to take responsibility for it. For this, bodies are needed, as physical existence makes it possible to conclude, for example: the reason I am not happy is that my sexual life is not right, or I do not even have a sexual life; or I am unhappy because I was sexually abused as a child. These are not the reasons we are unhappy, however. Instead, the cause lies in our choice against the Holy Spirit. Incidentally, this does not mean that we should not seek professional help, nor ignore the effects of abuse, etc. Since we believe we are bodies, help almost always needs to begin where we believe we are. In the end, though, we must come to recognize that true healing occurs only in the mind, for that is all there is. I shall return to this issue of behavioral change presently.

Every experience in the world fulfills this underlying wish of our ego self to retain the separation we stole from God, but to blame everyone else for it, which means blaming the body: I blame your body for what it has done to me; I blame my body for how it has failed me; I blame my parents' bodies for their adverse effect on me; I blame my bodies in former lifetimes for how they adversely affected me; I blame the genetic structure I have inherited. The form of the accusation does not matter, since the content of the wish remains the same.

Another factor that reflects the origins of sex is its association with violence, whether in the extreme form of rape or incest, or the more subtle forms of psychological violence. In the ego's myth, the original separation thought was violent—the rape of Heaven. This, of course, has nothing to do with reality or the true God, Who knows nothing of any of this. Yet once the ego began weaving its nightmarish myth of what we did to God, and what He will do in return, it convinced us that we had committed an unimaginably heinous sin, despicable and unpardonable: we raped and violated our Source, wresting in righteous wrath (T-23.II.11:2) what in our insanity we believed belonged to us; we took God's Life and His creative power, so we now have power over Him. This is why

deep down in everyone's mind—male or female—
there is the terrifyingly guilty thought: I am the original
rapist. With some people this manifests in the form of
physical rape, but deep down everyone is guilty of this
sin—just as deep down everyone is a Nazi, a terrorist,
and an evil-doer—all different terms for what the ego
told us occurred in the separation. And none of it ever
happened at all!

Thus are we all born into this world with over-
whelming guilt. Indeed, Jesus tells us that the world
"is the delusional system of those made mad by guilt"
(T-13.in.2:2). Therefore, how could anything of the
body *not* be infused with this abiding sense of sin?
Once again, sex, because of its unique place in human
life—physically and psychologically, individually and
societally—is uniquely qualified to be the repository
of our guilt and of problems with violence and pleasure, with separation, exclusivity, and specialness.

Sex as a Classroom

Once we understand that problems with sex, as
with all other problems, are not what they seem, there
is hope. We no longer have to attempt to solve a problem that has no solution. That is the hope offered by
the first principle of miracles, which may be restated:
There is no order of difficulty in healing. The problem

is one, as is the solution: belief in separation, undone by belief in Atonement. Accordingly, our need is to avail ourselves of the Answer in our minds. Here is where sex can serve a mighty purpose, and this is now our focus.

Our starting point is life in the body, where we believe we are. Within the ego's system, the foundation of existence is our embodying the thought of guilt, condemned and compelled to be repeated—to borrow Freud's concept of *repetition compulsion*—as the mistake that got us here in the first place: the ongoing desire to separate from God and destroy His Love, cannibalizing it to make it our own as we violently overthrow Heaven to satisfy our self-centered need to exist.

Unbeknownst to us, we act out this violent thought in our everyday lives, and indeed, go through life reinforcing this guilt over and over, until at some point we throw up our hands in desperation and cry out: "There must be another way." The pain of living in the body becomes too great, not just in terms of sexual issues, but in the conflict surrounding just about every activity. As we grow older, more rapidly than we would like, our bodily needs demand more and more attention. The body never worked perfectly to begin with, but over the years it becomes increasingly imperfect, and we realize that nothing in the world helps in any significant way because the problems are never truly resolved. As I mentioned earlier, referring to workbook lessons 79 and 80, no sooner do we solve one problem than another rises to take its place. This futile process goes on and on, until we recognize our need for another Teacher. By asking Him for help, our lives are transformed into classrooms of learning.

At first our lives are perceived as prisons, in which we magically hope to imprison others so we will be free. These others became the guilty sinners whom God will punish. However, these same enemies now become our saviors, for we have turned to the wise, egoless Presence within, referred to in *A Course in Miracles* as the Holy Spirit or Jesus, although any symbol will work as long as it reflects this non-judgmental Presence of love. The help we receive is unique, for it teaches us how to look differently at the world, and specifically our individual relationships, showing us that they can serve a different purpose. This help is not directed at having us do things in the world, but at changing how we perceive it. Moreover, the most effective learning situations are those that contain the most conflict, fear, and anxiety—all aspects of specialness—because they bring out the mind's deepest recesses of guilt, which we now experience as bodies. Jesus helps us understand that our experiences as bodies in the dream are nothing but projections of a life we made real in our minds. And this inner life is itself a defense against the real problem of the decision maker's misuse of its power of choice.

Every time we come to Jesus for help, his answer will be that what we experience outside is a projection of what we have made real inside: the world is "the outside picture of an inward condition" (T-21.in.1:5) —*projection makes perception*. We first look within and see the ego's thought system of separation and guilt. Making that reality, we project it in the illusory hope that it will no longer be in us but in someone else, thereby freeing us of its painful presence. Once again, all our external problems and concerns come from the ego's maladaptive attempts to remove a problem that is itself unreal.

By choosing to learn the thought system Jesus teaches us, we have a context in which to place our everyday experiences. It is most important that we focus on these experiences, and not do a metaphysical trip on ourselves and think that because the Course teaches the world and body are illusions, that we believe it. We must begin where we believe we are—in the body—otherwise Jesus cannot teach us. Thus we need to focus on whatever goes on in our daily lives. To restate it, the classrooms are these lives, and special relationships—with our body and those of others— constitute the curriculum our new teacher uses to instruct us. We therefore need to see sex as part of that curriculum, whether we are sexually active or not—

not because sex is any better or worse than anything else in our lives, but because it is such a significant part of our classroom in this physical world. In this way, Jesus can help us recognize that what we experience in terms of the body is the shadowy fragment of what we made real in the mind.

It cannot be said enough that knowing the meta-physical underpinnings of the Course's thought system is most helpful, because they provide the framework within which we can make sense of our lives, giving them a mighty purpose. What the mind does with sexuality has intention, as with every aspect of our bodily experience. Until now, the body had the negative goal of proving that separation is real, the same goal shared by the specifics of victimization and the pleasure-pain continuum. One of sexuality's purposes, therefore, was to prove that something outside the mind gives pleasure and happiness. A major myth about sexuality, moreover, has been that it will make us whole and complete—in heterosexual behavior, for example, male and female come together and become one. Indeed, Plato taught in his great myth that in the beginning we were androgynous—both male and female—and then became separated. This kind of thinking, then, becomes the ego's justification for finding union through the body. On the other hand, sexuality can also be the source of sin and guilt, shame and fear, wherein religions have found justification for their belief in sexual abstinence as a key to spiritual advancement. Either position misses the point, for true unholiness and holiness have their locus only in the mind, where the decision for the ego or Holy Spirit is made.

This underscores the importance of the line I quoted earlier: "Minds are joined; bodies are not" (T-18.VI.3:1). What joins you with another person is not copulation, but shared purpose. This can be expressed in a sexual relationship or a non-sexual one. It can be expressed anywhere, anytime. As Jesus says at the beginning of the manual, you may be riding on an elevator when a child bumps into you, but you do not judge the child (M-3.2). In that holy instant you do not see the child as separate from you. This is the meaning of *joining*.

More than anything else, therefore, sex is a classroom of joining, reflecting the learning that occurs in the mind. If, for example, you have used sex as an instrument of separation or exclusion, of gaining pleasure at another's expense, satisfying your needs without caring for the other, it can be a powerful classroom—not because of anything inherent in the sexual behavior *per se*, but because of the way you have misused it. This is no different from using food as a form of self-abuse, which means that food can be a powerful symbol of learning to be kind and gentle to yourself. Clearly, then, learning has nothing to do with sexual or eating behavior, but with the purpose your mind has given it. Similarly, if you have used living space as a means of reinforcing separation, exclusion, and victimization, or as a special substitute for your home in Heaven, that, too, becomes a wonderful learning vehicle for you, learning to look at houses or apartments differently. Finally, if you have used cars as a way of self-aggrandizement, as people sometimes do—a way of boasting about how strong, rich, and wonderful you are; or, conversely, of your poverty, misery, and unworthiness—then cars assume the potential of becoming important symbols of forgiveness.

Remember that the ego speaks first and is always wrong (T-5.VI.3:5; 4:2). When it speaks, it speaks in thought, because *everything* is thought. And thought is projected into form—"All thinking produces form at some level" (T-2.VI.9:14)—for whatever is of the wrong mind is projected, as God's Love in the Mind is always extending. Yet this extension is not of time or space, and cannot be understood in our separated state. This is true of guilt as well, except that guilt projects instead of extends. Thus love extends and guilt projects—the fundamental law of mind. In truth, there is only one ego thought—separation—which fragmented when the thought was projected. While it appears that we project multitudinous forms, we all share the same fundamental thought that has never left its source in the Son's one mind.

Just as "all roads lead to Rome," all external roads lead to guilt—the seat of the ego's power. The individual meanings of our roads differ; for example, sex may symbolize sin and damnation for one, while expressing holiness and love for another. That is why it is important not to judge another's behavior—their classrooms and curricula. *Content is the same; forms differ.* And so whatever we have used to keep us separate and special, the Holy Spirit uses to teach us a different content—forgiveness instead of guilt.

The ego has convinced us that the basic problem is our inherent incompletion or lack—the *scarcity principle*. This is the heart of the special relationship, and so is the heart of the ego thought system. The ego told us that when we separated from God something became terribly wrong, witnessed to by our guilt. The ego then took that one step further and said that what is wrong can never be corrected. We are sinful and guilty—"the home of evil, darkness, and sin" (W-pI.93.1:1). Yet the situation is not hopeless, the ego contends, for something can be done about this depressing feeling of lack and incompleteness: we merely take from the outside to complete ourselves.

This is Jesus' focus in "The Choice for Completion" (T-16.V), one of the text's more important sections on special relationships. Both the ego and Holy Spirit provide us with a choice of what will complete us. The ego offers us the special relationship to make us whole, while the Holy Spirit offers Atonement. He thus agrees with the ego that something is indeed missing in us; except what the Holy Spirit knows to be the truth is not really missing at all, merely hidden and craftily concealed by the ego's strategy of mindlessness. Therefore, our completion does not come through external joining, but through joining with the One Who reflects the completion of Heaven. This internal completion—the love that is the completion of Heaven —automatically extends throughout our mind, and around the world that has never left its source.

As we have emphasized, sex plays a major role in the ego's plan. It is almost universally believed that we cannot feel whole as a man or a woman without a sexual partner. Inevitably, then, success on that level can become an all-consuming quest. If it happens, we feel complete and whole—until the next day when we have to do it all over again—the aforementioned Don Juan complex wherein *one* is never enough. Completion through sex can never be enough, because it is always external. The same is true of hunger—the experience of lack in our stomachs. We fill them and are satisfied, until several hours later, if not several minutes later, when we have to eat again. At night we feel tired, so we have a good night's sleep and feel refreshed in the morning. Hours go by and we are tired all over again, needing to repeat the previous night's experience. Such is life in the body, and so the world is never enough; perhaps for now, but not later. Psychologically, of course, it works the same way. You may be loving, kind, thoughtful, and attentive to me now, but will that be the case in the future? I therefore continually have to entice you into my web of specialness so you will give me what I need to feel complete and whole.

Returning to our central point, it is important to divorce sex from spiritual connotations of any kind. Sex is a bodily activity—physical and psychological—like any other. What makes sex spiritual is its use—not its physical expression—the purpose of undoing the guilt of separation. This corrects the ego's investment in separate interests. Indeed, everything here has meaning only in terms of its ability to correct these ego mistakes. Yet the key to healing in the classroom of sexuality is understanding that in itself sex is nothing, because in itself the world is nothing. Only the mind's purpose confers meaning, and so only the mind can be healed.

Conclusion: Sex—Form and Content

Some students of *A Course in Miracles* have interpreted it to say that specialness is bad, meaning no one should be excluded from one's love, *and so one should have sex with everyone!* The ego, after all, is quite adept at adding two and two and getting five.

Thus, people believe they are being true to the Course by allowing everyone to enjoy the pleasure of their sexual company, for that is a way of living the lofty spiritual teaching of non-exclusion. The mistake here is rather clear: the confusion of form and content. *Specialness is content, not form.* You can no more make love to everyone than you can invite the world to your home for Christmas. Jesus speaks only of excluding people from your *thoughts*. By saying that a thought of love embraces everyone without exception, he means without condemnation, criticism, or judgment. Once again, it is essential to recognize that Jesus never speaks about behavior or the world of form, but only the mind.

Interestingly, this particular error is almost identical to the practice of many Gnostics in the early Christian centuries, although not those in the higher Gnostic schools. One of the key elements in Gnostic belief is that the world was not made by God. They would not have used the word *ego*, but the Gnostics were quite explicit about the world not being divine, and so the biblical God was a false deity. Some Gnostics had a vile hatred of the body and the world, and the worst thing imaginable was to think that God had anything to do with the body or the world. As a result, there were groups that believed that the way to prove they were not under the laws of this world (i.e., the ego)—which came from the *archons*: other-worldly powers that were not of God—would be to deliberately violate them. And guess what was number one on their list? As did some Course students almost two millennia later, they would have sex with anyone, invalidating the world's laws and proving they had transcended all obstacles to their lives as spirit.

It is therefore important to be alert to the mistake of confusing *form* (body) and *content* (mind). The ego is always interested in form to the exclusion of content, while Jesus is interested only in content, and to him once the dream was established, the form became neutral. Recall the lesson near the end of the workbook that says, "My body is a wholly neutral thing" (W-pII.294), for it can serve the purpose of either the ego or Holy Spirit.

Whenever you are tempted to think some things in the world can bring you closer to God or drive you to hell, know that you are subscribing to the ego's first law of chaos—there is a hierarchy of illusions (T-23.II.2). You say the world has power; e.g., sex can drive you to hell because of its evil and sinful nature, or take you to Heaven because it expresses your unity with God. Yet sex is nothing because everything here is nothing. The world is nothing because there is no world, being only a projection. The purpose determined by the mind gives things and events their meaning, not the world itself. This is what Jesus teaches in the early workbook lessons, a vital part of our training: Nothing in the world means anything because *we* have given everything here its meaning; by having it appear there is a meaningful world outside the mind, the ego proves the separation is real.

Think of Hamlet's famous line: "for there is nothing either good or bad, but thinking makes it so" (II,ii). There is nothing inherently right or wrong about the world, the body, or any activity here. Only our thinking makes it so. As soon as you think an activity is particularly harmful, evil, or wrong, or particularly helpful, holy, and right, you but make it real, which is the ego's strategy of keeping us mindless. If you make the world real in your experience or theology, if you give power to anything in the world, you are falling into the ego's trap by giving the world a reality it does not have. And this, then, is the purpose behind behavior. It is not that sex is wonderful or abhorrent—the ego does not care either way, whether you see the body as a source of pleasure or pain—as long as you think it is *something*, and thus make a big deal about it.

Many of you know Krishnamurti's line about sex: "Do it or don't do it, but get on with it." In other words, stop making it into a big deal. Sex is like anything else. We do not stop and ask whether or not we should breathe. We simply breathe. Sex is really no different. It is a biological fact that everyone has sexual feelings. From this point of view, sex is like any other bodily activity: Do it or don't do it, but get on with it. There is nothing in *A Course in Miracles* that says you should have an active sexual life; there is nothing in *A Course in Miracles* that says you should not. There is nothing in the Course about it at all. Jesus, I assure you, does not care what you do with your body. He cares very much, though, what you do with your mind—whether you choose him or the ego as your teacher. If he cared about the body he would be in a lot of trouble, as would we. The Jesus of the gospels does care, however, which has become a source of much pain in the world. Christians have continually confused form and content, failing to recognize that everything is in the mind, in which there are but two thoughts: separation and exclusion, unity and inclusion. Bodies cannot join together, but minds do. In fact, minds are already one, and so in truth need not even join.

As students of *A Course in Miracles*, therefore, we are asked to release all barriers reflecting separation that keep the mind in a state of sin and guilt. Once in that state, we automatically project the mind's content and make our bodies into symbols of separation and exclusion.

* * * * * * * * * *

Q: I understand that we cannot fix our problems through changing the form, but aren't there some situations where you have to stop a behavior before you can get to the deeper level of content? Take someone who is drinking himself to death; he has to quit drinking before he will ever get an answer to the real problem.

A: Absolutely. In the early weeks of the scribing, Jesus told Helen he was not against behavioral discipline. However, a change in behavior, if it is genuine, would have to reflect a change in *thinking*. Since addictions reflect our decision for the ego—a decision for specialness—drinking, or any other self-destructive behavior, becomes a symbol of the choice for guilt. When we engage Jesus as our teacher and ask for help with our curriculum—in this case, alcoholism—the real help is on the level of content. In other words, Jesus helps us with what our drinking symbolizes. And so our giving up drinking—or any addictive behavior—does not have to do with giving up drinking as such, but symbolizes giving up the ego. It takes the form of alcohol because that is the form in which we expressed our love affair with the ego. The form does not necessarily change—the focus is still on alcohol—but the content or purpose changes. Again, our giving up the behavior reflects our giving up the ego, as our taking it on reflected our choosing the ego. Importantly, since we identify ourselves as bodies, we must remain within that symbolism to be helped. Remember that Jesus needs a curriculum and classroom in which he can teach. As we have seen, the Holy Spirit does not take away our special relationships, but changes their purpose and thus transforms them.

It is entirely possible that when the purpose changes, the behavior will change, and you would not experience a sense of loss if the transition has been right-minded. The problem with many addictions is that people give them up on the level of form without changing teachers, and thus they either return to the addictive behavior a week, month, or years later, or they find another addiction. For example, people may give up alcohol or sexual addictions, but become addicted to diet-Pepsi or religion instead. One can be said to be less injurious than the other, but the guilt remains in place nonetheless. Therefore, while on the one hand, it would be a positive step to give up alcohol and abusive sexual behavior, and have a soft drink or practice abstinence instead, you really want to give up your dependence on the ego. Working within the world of symbols—our home as bodies— becomes an essential part of the Holy Spirit's program to heal our minds.

Q: The beginning of the text talks about how physical aids are sometimes helpful because the worst thing you can do is add fear to fear.

A: Yes, that is where Jesus teaches that it is not a sin to take medicine (T-2.IV.4-5). And it is not a sin if you stop drinking or any other addiction. However, the point, again, is that addiction on the level of content will not stop until you change from guilt to forgiveness. Giving up the addiction on the level of behavior is a good first step, but as Jesus would say in *The Song of Prayer*, you want the whole song, not just a piece of it; you want to go to the top of the ladder, not just climb one or two rungs above the bottom (see S-1.I).

Q: Doesn't that come only when you are ready for it?

A: Of course. And we need to begin where we think we are. For that reason, I usually recommend to all those with addictive behavior, regardless of its form, that they enter some kind of treatment program to help rid themselves of the addiction. However, if they truly want to be healed, they must continue with the process, which means healing the mind. Giving up the addiction on the level of behavior can be an important first step so that they would be clear enough to begin working on the underlying issues of guilt and projection. Again, discipline is never a bad thing, unless it becomes harsh and punitive. Remember that since the ego made form

56

as the means of avoiding content, it is that same form that Jesus uses to lead us back to content—*his*. If we deny the one, we are effectively denying the other.

Q: Are you saying that before I have sex I should spend a few minutes meditating or thinking about my purpose in having sex?

A: Heavens, no! Would you meditate or think about your purpose before having dinner, or taking a shower? Try to be normal, and do what normal people do. Sex should be an issue only if there is conflict surrounding it, and if there is, ask Jesus to remind you that the problem is not what it seems, as we have been saying. Focusing on sex, as in your idea of meditation or thinking about it before entering the bedroom, can very easily turn into looking in the wrong place for the source of the conflict—the body instead of the mind. And then magically hoping that meditation will help you.

Therefore, try to see sex as just another classroom in which you are inviting Jesus to instruct you—not in *form*, but *content*. He will help you see your concerns as projections of the mind's decision to exclude love, leaving you feeling guilty and unworthy of it. Looking at purpose, then, means realizing the ego's investment in keeping you focused on the guilt experienced in the body, rather that your mind's decision to make guilt real.

3. Money

Introduction

Our understanding of the phenomenon of money —certainly in our society—is rooted in the ego's fundamental and now-familiar principle of *one or the other*. At the beginning, as one Son, we said to God: "You have something I want, and since You will not give it to me, I will take it—I will have it and You will not." In the simplest of terms, this principle states that if I have something, you lack it; and if you have it, I lack it. It cannot be that we both have it. For example, though we may both have a thousand dollars, we cannot have the same thousand dollars. That principle of *one or the other*—separate interests—begins the ego's dream, from which everything emanates. This is the key to understanding what goes wrong with our use of money, and how that misuse can be corrected and undone.

This central ego concept of separate interests is that we both cannot have the same thing—either God is God, or I am God, but there can be only one Creator. In truth, we are co-creators with God, but God remains First Cause and we His Effect. Strictly speaking, of course, in Heaven's perfect Oneness there can be no first or second, and Jesus teaches us that God is first in the Holy Trinity, without a second (T-14.IV.1:7-8; T-25.I.5:1-3)—i.e., no Father, Son, and Holy Spirit as defined in Christian theology—only God. In the ego framework, however, God is number one and we are number two, a totally unacceptable situation. In our dream we rebel and usurp God's place, leaving us on top. This is the core of the ego's reality, the content of the separated mind: I took life from God, and so I have it and He does not. Yet now I fear He will take it back from me, leaving me life-less—the foundational thought we project and re-live in every special relationship.

Within the ego's system, to repeat, lack is paramount—the *scarcity principle* we discussed above—with its cardinal principle being *one or the other*. Therefore, when we made up a world as a defense against the threatening content in our minds, we made scarcity an integral part of the system—some have what others lack. Thus, the body, as I noted in our discussion of sex, was made to be the instrument of scarcity. If I do not fill my lungs with oxygen, my body with food and water, and my psychological body with love and attention, something terrible will surely happen. The nature of the body is such that it is perpetually in a state of lack or need—a veritable need machine—because our ontological origin is a thought of lack and need.

To recap, the ego devised a strategy that brilliantly keeps its wish to maintain our separation, but have someone else be blamed for it. This is what is experienced as lack in the world, where we automatically look to hold someone else accountable for our miserable state. Indeed, whatever the need, someone is *always* responsible, for the ego will never let us look at our own part in our condition. In the ego world, then, *scarcity* inevitably leads to the belief in *deprivation*, described in the ego's fourth and fifth laws of chaos (T-23.II.9-13). This is a critical piece in the ego's strategy, for if someone is going to deprive us, there has to be someone there. In other words, a world of separate individuals is necessary to justify the projections of responsibility for our scarcity. This also means that we want others to have more than we do, because that allows us to declare that we have been unfairly treated.

This is what is behind Jesus' emphatic warning: "Beware of the temptation to perceive yourself unfairly treated" (T-26.X.4:1). Deprivation is a powerful temptation because as long as I believe I am unfairly treated—not difficult to do in our world—I am off the hook. Moreover, my unhappiness, misery, and poverty clearly demonstrate there is an *I* who feels these things, and yet it is not my fault. Once again, I get to keep my ego's cake and eat it, too. The more I suffer, the better my ego likes it; and so within my mind I want to live in a world of inequality. Indeed, the world *is* a state of inequality because it has not left its source of inequality, which ultimately rests on the perception that God has the power and I do not. This is a battlefield, and the unequal conditions are perceived by the ego as unfair. God is God, and He is going to destroy me even though I believe I destroyed Him.

The ego thought system of scarcity and deprivation projects itself and makes a world that expresses the same inequality. In such a world we live with separate interests, and the symbolism of money emerges from that. My interests are clearly separate from yours because I want to live at your expense, and you want to live at mine. One could not ask for more dichotomous interests, for these mutually exclusive goals cannot be achieved at the same time. The world must be this way because, again, its source is the ontological thought that God and I have competing interests. He thinks He is God and I think I am; I want to destroy Him and He feels likewise. Yet only one of us will survive—*kill or be killed*. This thought is so horrific that all we could ever do is run from it, accomplished by burying the thought in our minds and covering it with the world, protected by the veil of forgetfulness.

All we are aware of now is the universe of inequality in which our bodies live, wherein one experience of

victimization follows another. This explains our being born as helpless infants, innocent victims of the
world around us. As a result, it is not my fault that I
am unhappy: it is not my fault that I was born, that my
mother drank while she was carrying me, was taking
cocaine, or had AIDS; it is not my fault that I was not
fed when I was hungry; fate was certainly cruel when
I was born into poverty, midst the wealth of other
families—*it is not my fault*. There is, of course, not a
person who would not agree with this estimation of
an unfair world. Yet it is only the ego thought underlying these experiences that is unfair.

Money as the Inequality of Specialness

One of the world's great symbols of inequality is
money. Some have it, others do not. And most people
make it at another's expense. The recent corporate
scandals are flagrant examples, but these are hardly
unusual. Typically—and there are always exceptions
—people running businesses seek to make money,
and if they are shrewd, they will spend as little as
possible on the product and get as much as they can
through its sale. This is seen as normal in capitalism,
even where there is no abuse of the system. We do not
really care what others get, as long as we get what we

want. Excesses of the system abound, and include re-
placing people with machines, looking overseas or to
illegal, vulnerable, or underage populations to exploit
workers for greater profit, and inflating employer sal-
aries at the expense of worker benefits. Not everyone
runs a company like that, of course, but it certainly
seems to be the norm because interests are separate:
the customer wants the best product possible; the
business person needs to sell it to make a profit. Each
is trying to get the best deal, and so, inevitably, there
are conflicting interests. Given its source in the ego
thought system, such practice of separate interests is
inherent in the human condition.

We live in a world in which a very small percentage of the people have the most money, while the
greater percentage live below the poverty level. This
should come as no surprise, for the situation simply
reflects how and why the world was made, which, to
state it once again, was to take the mind's thought system of inequality, injustice, scarcity, and power, and
project it so it would not be seen and corrected. The
question should not be how this could happen, but
how we could fail to recognize that this is the situation. Thus the importance of understanding the ego,
especially the concept of *projection*. Familiarity helps
one see how what is inside appears to be outside; and,
further, that whatever is perceived must first come
from within. The content must be the same, for *ideas*

leave not their source. As the text states, in a passage
from which we have already partially quoted:

> Projection makes perception. The world you
> see is what you gave it, nothing more than that.
> But though it is no more than that, it is not less…
> It is the witness to your state of mind, the outside
> picture of an inward condition. As a man thinketh,
> so does he perceive (T-21.in.1:1-3,5-6).

Money is not ordinarily seen as an instrument to
express shared interests. Instead, it almost always expresses the thought system of separate interests. Consequently, most people want as much money as they
can possibly get. Perhaps some think it is for altruis-
tic reasons: I want it for my family, my business, my
not-for-profit organization that does humanitarian
work. Yet almost always it is about *my* family, *my*
business, *my* organization, *my* pride and reputation—
not a collective and universal *our*.

Most relationships are developed on that basis, as
the Course's principles on special relationships teach.
I want something from you—your love, attention,
adulation—whatever I need. I do not really care about
you, even though my words may claim that. I want
what you have because there is something lacking in
me. Indeed, I particularly resent having to come to
you, for what I need was originally mine and you took
it. That is why you have it and I do not. Remember,

scarcity leads to deprivation. The special relationship is set up so that I need to bargain in order to get the love and attention I require. I therefore figure out how to meet your needs—albeit as minimally as I can—in order for you to feel that you are getting something from me, in exchange for what you will give in return.

The passages on special love relationships are perhaps more disturbing than any others in *A Course in Miracles* because they hit so close to home—the ego's thought system we never want to see again. They reveal what goes on beneath the surface of specialness, and it is not a pretty picture. The ugly essence of the special relationship is that I have given you something I know is of no value: *me*. If I really were of value and worth something, I would not need you to supply my lack. And so I trade my little self, which I have already judged to be nothing, and dress it up in a beautiful box with gorgeous wrapping, tied with a bright ribbon and bow. I pretend I am giving you this wonderful gift when I truly know there is nothing inside the box. I hope and pray you will not notice, that being so enamoured of the beautiful wrapping you never open the box or, to switch to the metaphor of "The Two Pictures," you will be so attracted to the frame of specialness that you will never notice the picture of death contained within it (T-17.IV). In this exchange, again—the core dynamic of specialness—I get what I value, giving you something of little or no worth.

Rarely do both parties in a business deal sit down and amicably and honestly discuss what is needed on both sides, and then proceed to negotiate on that basis. Almost always, as I have been saying, each wants to get as much as he can and give as little as possible for it. Labor unions arose to correct management abuse, but as history has shown, they, too, fell into the same temptation of abuse of power. If shared interests were the reigning principle, employer and employee would need nothing more than a hand shake of inherent equals sitting around a coffee table. Unfortunately, however, money has become the great vehicle for this dynamic of separation, an enormous symbol of the power of meeting one's interests at another's expense. It becomes the policy not only of individuals, but of governments, rogue governments, and groups of various kinds. For example, rulers wanting to remain in power have been known to keep their subjects/citizens impoverished and dependent, thereby reducing chance of rebellion. And, of course, they require huge defenses and defenders to protect their interests.

We return to the central principle of specialness—giving little and receiving much—and take a short detour by seeing this dynamic at work in the practice of religion. Once the scenario of separation began to unfold, we tried to buy God off, which gave rise to formal religions. These represent the attempt to purchase God's Love, which is the thought behind Jesus' response to the question of the role of religion in psychotherapy: "Formal religion has no place in psychotherapy, but it also has no real place in religion" (P-2.II.2:1). By formal religion, Jesus means the ordinary practice of Hinduism, Buddhism, Judaism, Christianity, and Islam—not their more spiritual or mystical forms of expression. The forms or rituals establish the rules of bargaining with God, with money often their most prominent symbol. Think of the strange idea of tithing: God has given us the gift of love and life, and now we must give Him one-tenth of our earnings. In this bargain there is always an element of sacrifice. If we are honest with ourselves, we would acknowledge that part of us bitterly resents having to sacrifice—that we have to pay for love—because on some level we believe everything should be given us. This dynamic, incidentally, may also take the form of saying: "Because I have been so blessed, I want to give something back in return." This denies the fact that we all have been blessed with everything. Confusing form and content remains the prime characteristic of the ego's thought system as it is expressed in the world.

The ego is about power. Having acquired it in our dream of separation, we made a world in which we became masters of life and death. Money has come to symbolize that power, based upon the principle of separate interests that originated in the distorted view of our relationship with the Creator. As an illustration, say we have amassed a large amount of money or have acquired all the material goods we could ever want. Yet something still grates on us and we are not entirely peaceful. The reason is that on some level we realize that we stole the money and possessions we amassed. Even if acquired honestly, the ego would always accuse us of stealing. It must be so because our original acquisition—individual existence—was stolen from God, and so, following from its fourth law of chaos, the ego tells us that whatever we have, we took from another—*you have what you have taken* (T-23.II.9:1-4).

The world may not look at it that way, but we do, because we got what we wanted, reminding us of the ontological instant when we got what we wanted at God's expense. Since time is not linear and everything has happened at once, what is true in the past must be true in the present. Guilt is inevitably built into our lives and gnaws at us from within. Thus, no matter how many possessions we may have, a feeling persists that it is never enough. We need more and more because we must cover our guilt. This was the basis of John Calvin's doctrine that you know you are part of God's elect if you are materially successful, and in other ways as well, and are not part of the elect if you are a failure in life. By believing that God wants us to have wealth, money becomes spiritualized. The other side is portrayed in the Bible, where money is seen as the root of all evil—you cannot worship God and Mammon, for it has to be *one or the other*. As a result, many people conclude that they cannot be spiritually acceptable to God if they are wealthy, the opposite side of the coin that is expressed in Calvinism, which makes materiality the holy Will of God.

Money and Guilt

As with sex, money has guilt built into it because it is based on scarcity—*one or the other*—and the abuse of power. In that they share the common purpose of making guilt and the body real, money and sex are no different. How could they be, since both are based on separate interests? If I have money, then to my ego this means some people do not have it. If *everyone* made money in the stock market, or bet and won on the same horse in a race, the marketplace and horse racing could not survive. Some people must win and others lose. Yet when we do win, the unconscious thought of guilt inevitably follows: "My God, I did it again; stealing and killing to get what I wanted." Everything reminds us of the original thought and its consequences. Recall this line: "Think not He has forgotten" (M-17.7:4).

God remembers, and *will* exact His punishment. One way of dealing with guilt is to cover it with more and more money, just as anxious people try to quell their anxiety with more and more food, as if the source of ego thoughts and feelings resided in an empty wallet or stomach. Near the end of "The Anti-Christ," Jesus speaks of this ego characteristic:

> Each worshipper of idols harbors hope his special deities will give him more than other men possess. It must be more. It does not really matter more of what; more beauty, more intelligence, more wealth, or even more affliction and more pain (T-29.VIII.8:6-8).

Any form of defense will do, as long as it reinforces the specialness that distinguishes me from everyone else.

As it can be difficult to have a sexual relationship without guilt, so it is difficult to have money without guilt intruding in some way. Yet there is nothing inherently right or wrong about money. As with sex, the source of guilt is the ego purpose that money serves: the need for separate interests, and then its justification. Remember Hamlet's wise observation: "There is nothing good or bad, but thinking makes it so." Earning money is not good, nor is it bad. It simply depends on *what it is for*. If in any way you are making money at another's expense, or are being dishonest in your dealings, your business might thrive, but so will your guilt—the ego's hidden purpose from the beginning.

It thus behooves us as students of *A Course in Miracles* to ask Jesus' help to look at what our business practices might be: seeing not only potential customers as inherently adversarial, but employees as well—all with interests apart from our own; deceptive advertising, inserting fine print in contracts to trick consumers, or efficiently controlling costs, yet maintaining or even increasing prices to maximize profits; reducing quantities and/or quality of items without reducing prices, thereby having consumers pay the same or more while receiving less— in this regard, one clever strategy has been to decrease slightly the size of a box or container, yet keeping (or even raising) the cost to the consumer, or, even more sneakily, keeping the same size, but reducing the actual amount of the product contained within. While it is true that corporations by law are obligated to their shareholders to make money as best they can, maximizing profits on the level of form does not preclude an *attitude* of sharing, wherein the public is not being deceived or taken advantage of, nor are the employees exploited for the benefit of "the bottom line." Looking at these practices openly and honestly leads to awareness of which teacher had been hired as our business consultant.

Eventually we reach the point when the pain of guilt becomes intolerable. Having everything we want is still not enough, or the counterpart, agonizing over never having what we want—and so we say: "There must be another way." This is the invitation to Jesus to become our teacher and guide, and allows him to teach us that the problem is not the money itself—its presence *or* absence—but our attitude toward it. Again, the super wealthy and the super poor are opposite sides of the same coin, for they both derive great benefit from their situations. Those *with* money cannot avoid the guilt over stealing, while those *without* money cannot avoid the guilt that comes from pointing an accusing finger, saying they lack money because the world has deprived them of it. Yet the point one day comes to all of us when we ask for help, and Jesus' response is to help us understand that we but re-enact the original thought of power and its abuse, of scarcity and deprivation. In other words, he teaches us to see that our financial situation reflects the ego's thought system of separate interests—*one or the other.*

Jesus clearly wants us to learn how much happier we would be if we led our lives based on his principle of shared interests. In fact, he has told us that this is the only qualification for being a teacher of God (M-1.1:2). If one person loses or is deprived of anything, the entire

Sonship loses because it is one. If we attempt to make meaningful distinctions among the seemingly separate members of the Sonship, we but crucify God's Son—*again*. It cannot be that someone loses and we win, or that we lose and another wins. Chapters 25 and 26 in the text especially deal with the question of justice, and Jesus says the rock on which salvation rests is that no one loses and everyone gains (T-25.VII.12). The ego's rock, on which its church is built, is that there must be sacrifice if one is to gain, leading to a world of winners and losers, haves and have-nots.

Since the world arose from the ego thought system of gain and loss, the only way it can change and economic disadvantage be alleviated is for people to change their minds—shifting from the ego's doctrine of separate interests to the Holy Spirit's vision of shared interests—realizing everyone is the same. This does not mean you must let go of money or possessions, anymore than you would give up sex. The Holy Spirit does not take away your special relationships; He transforms them (e.g., T-17.IV.2:3; T-18.II.6-7) by changing their purpose. This needs to be underscored in order not to confuse *A Course in Miracles* with other systems. Jesus is not saying that you should give away everything you feel is important to you, but that you would be happier giving away the thought system of which your possessions have been made the symbol. To restate this essential point, Jesus' teaching has nothing to do with behavior or setting aside your business skills, but only with the one with whom you do business—your ego or him—with whom you think about money. Money, therefore, can be just as much a symbol of love and sharing as of separation and scarcity. The former reflects the Holy Spirit's Atonement —we are not separate—while the latter expresses the ego's separation—*one or the other*.

The last section of *Psychotherapy*, "The Question of Payment," addresses the issue of money, specifically whether therapists should charge their patients. Jesus' answer, in effect, says money is neutral:

> …everything in this world [can] be used by the Holy Spirit to help in carrying out the plan. Even an advanced therapist has some earthly needs while he is here. Should he need money it will be given him, not in payment, but to help him better serve the plan. Money is not evil. It is nothing (P-3.III.1:2-6).

This does not mean there should be no exchange of money, goods, or services. It means there is no cost, meaning there is no loss: *no one loses and everyone gains*. Jesus makes the distinction between *payment* and *cost*. The former expresses the principle of shared interests, in the form that both parties need—for one it is money, for the other it is the service provided: "To give money where God's plan allots it has no cost" (P-3.III.2:7). The latter, however, expresses the ego's belief in sacrifice—one receives and another loses: "To withhold it [money] from where it rightfully belongs has enormous cost" (P-3.III.2:8).

Jesus' approach to this issue is similar to the ideal proposed by Karl Marx: *From each according to his ability; to each according to his need.* This 19th-century visionary believed that in a society, people should give what they are able to give, and receive what they need. Marx's principle, incidentally, should not be confused with some modern political systems that may call themselves Marxist, as his was a utopian ideal based on equality. In the 1920s, Freud insightfully wrote that Marxism would inevitably fail, not because of anything external, but because Marx and his followers did not recognize the inherent aggression and self-centeredness in homo sapiens. Freud was expressing that this ideal of people expressing shared interests—each giving and receiving without agendas—was naive. He wisely knew that greed, selfishness, and hate are in everyone, and so we all inevitably fall back on separate interests. Indeed, this is what gave rise to us—our parents, birthplace, and home. It cannot be until this underlying ego thought system is undone that the world will reflect the Holy Spirit's shared love, rather than the ego's divisive hate.

The issue, once again, is not whether having money is evil and lacking it is good, or vice versa (depending on one's value system), but the peace that is shared with everyone. Nor does it suggest that well-off people should divest their wealth among the poor. The point is that *before* you act in any way, you should first go within and ask for help that all interferences of guilt and specialness be gone. Only then will your actions be caring and loving—for all concerned. Freud's point was that since Marxism focused on the *external*, it ignored the *internal*—the unconscious ego thought system that alone determines our motivations and actions. This principle, of course, works for *all* behavioral issues. For example, you can be expressing the principle of shared interests and still negotiate a price with a car dealer, or shop for the best value for your money. However, you would lack the ego's killer instinct wherein the lower price or "successful" negotiation meant victory, calling to mind—albeit unconsciously—the original triumph over God: "I got something for nothing!"

It would thus be helpful, *before changing your behavior*, to step back with Jesus and look at how you have conducted yourself with money (or with sex) based on separate interests: Seek not to change your behavior, but choose to change your mind about your behavior (T-21.in.1:7). This means first that you *look*

—this itself is the change, because the ego never looks. Look without judgment or guilt at what you have done, with regard either to yourself or others. For example, "I never told the absolute truth on my income tax return because, after all, the government consists of a bunch of thieves, anyway." Setting aside any ethical issues regarding the Internal Revenue Service itself, with such an attitude guilt is inevitable, because you are saying others did this to you first, and so you are justified in doing it to them. We have already discussed business dealings, where as a purchaser you seek the best deal you can get, without thinking of the seller, while as a seller, your concern is with your profit and not your customers. Whether this practice is within the law or in violation of it, the ego content remains the same, and equal partnership and sharing is not an acceptable option.

To function in accord with the Holy Spirit's vision of shared interests we do not need another to agree with us, nor do we have to invite others to share in the principle, unless they are willing to do so, of course. This is a shift we make within ourselves. We should never lose sight of the all-important principle that what allows us to survive—indeed, what gave us all existence in the first place—is separate interests. We will instinctively fall back on this, whether we are involved with sex, money, or anything else. It is imperative to realize the cost involved in functioning this way: the principle of separate interests reinforces the original thought of separation, which reinforces the guilt that arose from it; this, in turn, reinforces the belief that the body is real. We need this conclusion to shield us from the guilt in the mind. Keeping the belief in separate interests operative—whether flagrantly or subtly—is the ego's extremely clever and insidious means of keeping its thought system intact, even while we are devoting our lives to this course. Yet even though money as well as sex have been used to reinforce separation, abuse of power, and separate interests, they can still become a helpful part of the curriculum, a wonderful means of our learning to forgive—*our special function*, the theme of the next chapter.

* * * * * * * * * * *

Q: I have a job in a company that is involved in practices that cheat customers in some of the ways you mentioned. Does this mean I should leave my job?

A: Not necessarily. Before you would make a decision to leave a company that engages in practices you judge as unfair, consider the following: In judging your employers, are you in fact committing the same "sin" you accuse them of? Their selfishness in thinking only of themselves—separate instead of shared interests—

expresses the ego's underlying thought system of separation. Yet in siding with the victims against the victimizers, you are yourself expressing the same thought system of separation—dividing the Sonship into those who sin and those who are sinned against.

This does not mean you stay in the job, however; but recall what Jesus asks of us: *If a brother asks something outrageous of you, do it* (T-12.III.4:1). Perhaps the outrageous thing asked of you is to remain with your ego-based employers, so as to offer the forgiveness they would not feel they deserve, offering it to yourself at the same time. Or perhaps it is to leave your job, but with the blessing of forgiveness on those you are leaving. Regardless of your behavior, you would still be offering and receiving the forgiveness we *all* seek.

4. Summary

"The Special Function"

As a way of summarizing our previous discussion, we look at some passages from the last part of "The Special Function" in Chapter 25 of the text. As we go through this material—which is non-specific, as is almost everything else in *A Course in Miracles*—think of Jesus' words in the context of sex and money, aspects of our lives we used to hurt and keep us separate, which now can be looked at differently. Our special function is thus accepting the Holy Spirit's correction for our mistaken choices for the ego, and so the guilt that was projected into form can be returned to the mind and forgiven. Asking the Holy Spirit's help, we look through His vision at our use of the body, and by seeing only the shared interests of the Sonship, what we made to harm through separation becomes the means of our healing. Sex and money, which expressed the ego's thought system of *one or the other*, are transformed in purpose to reflect the Holy Spirit's principle of *together, or not at all* (T-19.IV-D.12:8).

(4:1-3) Such is the Holy Spirit's kind perception of specialness; His use of what you made, to heal

instead of harm. To each He gives a special function in salvation he alone can fill; a part for only him. Nor is the plan complete until he finds his special function, and fulfills the part assigned to him, to make himself complete within a world where incompletion rules.

Incompletion rules in the world because everything here has come from a thought of scarcity and lack. We make ourselves complete, not through anything external—acquiring more and more bodies to worship at our shrine, or more and more money with which to build ourselves an altar dedicated to the god of material success—but by making the choice for the Teacher Who will help us heal our minds of the erroneous thought of incompletion. The special function the Holy Spirit gives us has nothing to do with specifics, such as activities around *A Course in Miracles* or various philanthropic causes. Rather, it relates to the curriculum we have set up—the special relationships in our lives that involve a person, possessions, money, food, alcohol, etc. Our special function, then, is to ask for help to shift the purpose of the relationship from the ego's, which is to keep separate, to the Holy Spirit's, which is to heal.

If I have an addiction, for example, my special function is to forgive the addiction and the people I hold responsible for it. I therefore forgive by not giving them a power they do not have; i.e., they cannot take the peace of God from me—only my decision can do that. If I have a special relationship with you—love or hate—forgiving that relationship becomes my special function. If I have had a special relationship with money—either not having it and being unfairly treated, or having a lot of it and wanting the power that goes with it—that becomes the symbol I use in learning to forgive.

(5:1-2) Here, where the laws of God do not prevail in perfect form, can he yet do *one* perfect thing and make *one* perfect choice. And by this act of special faithfulness to one perceived as other than himself [the special love or hate partner], he learns the gift was given to himself, and so they must be one.

The "*one* perfect choice" is to forgive, rather than to make specialness real. Say you have a special relationship with money, which means you believe that your happiness and peace of mind depend on it. In back of that need for money would be a person, someone whom you felt had deprived you in the past. As a reaction to that, you may have determined to grow up and show how powerful you have become in spite of him or her. That is the person you have to forgive. It is not money; money is nothing. You have simply used money as a symbol of attack. From the other direction, if your parents deprived you and made you feel terrible as a child, you would show them how deprived you still are, and that it is all their fault. Consequently, you would go through life never having enough of anything.

These are merely opposite sides of the same coin. There will always be faces associated with the object of our addiction, whether we are addicted to a substance, sex, food, or money—it does not matter. The addiction could be positive or negative—having an abundance or lack of it—yet, again, there is a face behind the suffering that comes with the addiction. Almost always it is of our parents, but others would do just as well. And then we learn the gift of forgiveness was given to ourselves, and so we must be one. It must be so because our interests are one: special partners in separation become special partners in remembering our oneness—first as separated Sons, and then as one Son.

(5:3-4) Forgiveness is the only function meaningful in time. It is the means the Holy Spirit uses to translate specialness from sin into salvation.

Jesus is not referring to a behavioral change or shift, but a change in mind. In fact, that is all Jesus ever talks about. He does not care about our behavior. How can he care about a body that he knows is nonexistent, a figure in a dream that is illusory? He cares only about the dreamer—the decision maker in the mind, the only focus of his teaching.

(5:5) Forgiveness is for all.

This is a major theme throughout *A Course in Miracles*, expressed in many different forms. No one can be exempt from our forgiveness, for if we exclude anyone, we affirm that the Sonship of God is not one, and once again we crucify His undivided Son. Helen's poem "The Gifts of Christmas" opens with the lines:

> Christ passes no one by. By this you know
> He is God's Son. You recognize His touch
> In universal gentleness. His Love
> Extends to everyone. His eyes behold
> The Love of God in everything He sees.
> (*The Gifts of God,* p. 95)

We know we are hearing the Holy Spirit's Voice, taking Jesus' hand, and looking through Christ's vision when our attitude towards one person does not exclude another. While behavior, including the involvement of sex and money, is necessarily limited in expression, it does not have to specifically exclude anyone by the judgment of separate interests. To restate what has been emphasized throughout this book, sexual activity and interest in money are not in themselves wrong-minded. It is their expressing the ego's goal of separate interests that is the problem, which needs to be undone through forgiveness of others and ourselves. And so forgiveness must be for all; otherwise it is for no one.

(5:6-10) But when it rests on all it is complete, and every function of this world completed with it. Then is time no more. Yet while in time, there is still much to do. And each must do what is allotted him, for on his part does all the plan depend. He *has* a special part in time for so he chose, and choosing it, he made it for himself.

The "special part in time" is our ego's specialness. We wanted to be special, and so we were, because it is our dream. Note that Jesus says: "Yet while in time, there is still much to do." Even though time is an illusion, while we still believe we are in it there is the work of forgiveness to complete. We used time to reinforce its illusory nature, but given to the Holy Spirit the prison we made is transformed into a classroom within which we learn His lessons of forgiveness that undo the *past* of sin, the *present* of guilt, and the *future* of fear.

(5:11) His wish was not denied but changed in form, to let it serve his brother and himself, and thus become a means to save instead of lose.

Jesus really means changed in *content*. He is saying that our wish to be special has not been denied us, but now has a different meaning. Instead of our being special, exclusive, and separate, we learn we have a special function—to unlearn everything the ego taught us. Again, the ego's prison of specialness has become the Holy Spirit's classroom of forgiveness.

We skip to the next paragraph, sentence 6.

(6:6-8) The specialness he chose to hurt himself did God appoint to be the means for his salvation, from the very instant that the choice was made. His special sin was made his special grace. His special hate became his special love.

We chose our behavior regarding sex and money in order to hurt ourselves and/or others through specialness. In sentence 8, Jesus uses "special love" in a positive sense. We merely shift the purpose of what it means to be special. In order for us to make this shift, however, we must be aware of how we have abused power, money, sex, and all things of the body, which we did whenever we saw our interests as apart from another's. No one here escapes this ego principle, and feeling guilty is quite counter-productive. Indeed, we are in the world because we collectively did this with God at the beginning, or so we thought; and thus are we doomed to repeat it until we change our minds by changing our teacher.

We skip to the next paragraph, sentence 6.

(7:6) Only in darkness does your specialness appear to be attack.

We see our specialness as sinful only when we feel guilty about it, which constitutes the darkness. "Do not feel guilty," Jesus is saying. "Do not be concerned about the shadows, for that is why you came into the world [see T-18.IV.2]. From the ego's point of view, you were born to make the shadows real, and then blame everyone else for them. However, once here and realizing what you have done, you asked for help and thus allowed me to use your mistakes as classrooms to teach that you are forgiven. Only your guilt would teach that your specialness was a sin to be punished; but a mistake is not a sin. In fact, simply being born was a mistake, as was separating from God. Yet there is no hierarchy of mistakes, and it is merely silly, once it is seen, to hold on to the mistake through guilt instead of letting me help you undo it."

(7:7-10) In light, you see it as your special function in the plan to save the Son of God from all attack, and let him understand that he is safe, as he has always been, and will remain in time and in eternity alike. This is the function given you for your brother. Take it gently, then, from your brother's hand, and let salvation be perfectly fulfilled in you. Do this *one* thing, that everything be given you.

We need only join with Jesus in surveying our lives—past and present—and see our misuses of power, whether in relationships, with money, or in any other area. We then can say and mean: "Yes, this is what I have done, and I can see the pain it brought me, which I no longer want. I now know to whom I go to undo the guilt that is the source of my pain." This realization is all Jesus asks of us. It is enough.

Looking with Jesus

The question may yet remain, given the tension surrounding these high-energy subjects of sex and money, is it sufficient simply to look at them without doing anything more? The answer is an unqualified yes—we need only look at the seeming problem with Jesus, seeing the intensity and energy as part of the ego's strategy to root our awareness in externals. Recall that before I spoke specifically about sex and money, I read a line from the text about the insane belief that God would punish Jesus because of our sins; that although this was no different from any other illusion, it was more difficult to release because of its strong value as a defense. I used this as a lead-in to our discussion because it is so difficult to see sex and money as no different from other issues in our lives.

However, their emotional charge comes only from the projections of guilt onto the body, and it goes without saying that sex and money are almost totally body-oriented.

The ego made the body to keep us from getting back to our minds. The ego knows its existence is at stake, for if we should ever return to the mind, we would surely choose against the separation. The more intense our focus on the body, therefore—as in sex and money—the further removed we are from the mind. Moreover, both sex and money almost always reflect the ego's fundamental principle of *one or the other*. If I am to get what I want, achieve success, and attain pleasure and happiness, I must do so at someone else's expense. This is reminiscent of the original thought that it is either God or my self. If I am to exist—and I cherish my existence—God has to be sacrificed. This thought is the birth of our guilt that is omni-present in our minds, casting a shadow over the world's specific forms. Sex and money are simply two highly guilt-invested forms of this dynamic.

Yet it is precisely because of their prominence as defenses, susceptible to the projections of guilt, that sex and money become such powerful classrooms. Our object is merely to return to the mind's decision for guilt. If we do not, we can never be healed and will forever be mired in the depths of the ego's thought system, with no way out. The ego's strategy, of course, is to prevent this return by whatever means possible; not to let us become aware of guilt, yet still be directed by it. In this regard, anything that recalls to us the fact that we have a mind, suffused with guilt, is helpful.

Jesus therefore begins the process of healing by helping us see the ways we have been abused, or abused others in the name of sex or money. Having asked Jesus for help, we can view the intensity about sex and money as helpful red flags that tell us there is a serious problem, but it is not what we believed: "I am never upset for the reason I think" (W-pI.5). We cannot deny our conflict around these two areas, or that they have become preoccupations for us—the height of our special love or hate interests. Allowing ourselves to achieve this level of recognition inevitably leads to the next important step, which is getting in touch with the projections that fueled these issues. Sickness serves a similar purpose in the ego's strategy, as it, too, is a great preoccupation—when we are in pain, nothing matters but pain relief.

Again, the ego has used sex and money to rivet our attention to the world and the body, away from the mind. Yet when we finally throw up our hands in despair, saying, "Help, there must be another way of looking at this," the preoccupations that have been so essential to the ego's separation now become important aspects of the Holy Spirit's plan of Atonement.

The attention that was focused outside can now be turned inward, where we begin to realize that the problem we are experiencing outside is not really outside at all, but within the mind.

I mentioned earlier that Freud's insistence on his sexual theory was due largely to its roots in biology, which was of great importance to him. Biology means the body, and this helps us understand why we are so preoccupied, if not obsessed, with issues involving sex and money. These conflicted objects of our bodily preoccupation, again, help us get back to the real conflict, which has nothing to do with the physical. Using others to satisfy our needs—sexually or financially—is but the tip of the iceberg, which consists of the original "sin" of satisfying our need at God's expense: acquiring the individualized existence we craved by disposing of God. Our lives are nothing more or less than a series of variations on that primordial theme.

Consequently, we need to look at the intensity surrounding sex and money within this framework, as part of the ego's strategy to root attention in the body. In that sense it has served us remarkably well. The ego seeks always to make up problems where there are none. And the body and world were the ego's answer to what it defined as the problem of the mind—a battleground that would lead to our destruction. For this reason, the world was made to solve the problem of the mind's guilt, but then the world and body, with their multitudinous and complex components, became problems in their own right, demanding solutions— the more intense our experience of the problem, the more intently we focused on solving it on the bodily level: physically, psychologically, and socially. Yet once again the tables can be turned on the ego when we go to Jesus and look with him at the ego. He helps us understand that the intensity is not caused by the object outside, but by the enormity of the guilt and self-hatred inside. These in turn are defenses against the intensity of the love that defines us truly as Sons of God.

A section in the text is entitled, "The Attraction of Love for Love" (T-12.VIII), which points to the love where the real intensity is found, and which we seek to conceal:

> For still deeper than the ego's foundation, and much stronger than it will ever be, is your intense and burning love of God, and His for you. This is what you really want to hide (T-13.III.2:8-9).

Our yearning to go home is what the ego strives to stifle and conceal, resulting in the belief that our yearning is for the things in the world—love, comfort, and happiness, even for Heaven. Sex and money, the ego persuades us, are primary ways of fulfilling these yearnings. When we realize that the intensity connected with these bodily issues covers the intensity of the mind's abhorrent guilt, which covers the intensity of the mind's love, our lives take on a different light and our bodies a different purpose.

Looking with Jesus at these problems, therefore, means raising ourselves above the battleground and seeing the wider picture, realizing that the body is nothing more than the mind's projection. When seen that way, the intensity will diminish and eventually disappear, because what feeds it is the ego's purpose of keeping us focused outside. Indeed, the intensity must disappear because it is not fueled by the body—the body does not feel anything, our experience to the contrary. We talk about people having high sexual energy or high metabolism or high whatever, calling these biological facts. But there are no biological facts! The body feels what it is told to feel by the mind. And so, again, we do not have to change what the body feels; we but change the purpose the body's feelings were made to serve. For the ego, the purpose was to keep us mindless; for the Holy Spirit, the body becomes a way of returning us to the problem and becoming mindful.

We can therefore see that intensity is another of the ego's lines of defense, a way of riveting attention to the world, whether the intensity is about sex, money, food, making a name for oneself, or needing to be right and proving other people wrong. The intensity will diminish because it had been misplaced, being the ego's insane attempt to displace our intensity for God's Love onto something external. As we make the ongoing decisions to return home and forgive, there will be less need to defend against our guilt. Yet every once in a while the ego will rear its ugly head and a massive ego attack will ensue. That is when the ego becomes vicious, which occurs when we begin to take the Holy Spirit's evaluation of us more seriously (T-9.VII.4:4-7). Elsewhere, Jesus tells us the ego will become retaliative when we take his hand on the journey:

> Whenever fear intrudes anywhere along the road to peace, it is because the ego has attempted to join the journey with us and cannot do so. Sensing defeat and angered by it, the ego regards itself as rejected and becomes retaliative (T-8.V.5:5-6).

It is extremely helpful to understand this principle, so that when we become afraid and experience guilt or hate, we will understand what is going on and not have an ego attack over having had an ego attack.

To be clear, *A Course in Miracles* is not *against* sex or making money, but neither is it *for* them. Jesus does not care about any of this because the body is not real to him. Purpose alone is important, and purpose is found in the mind. *That* is his only concern. Jesus is in the mind and nowhere else, because *there is nowhere else*. Remember, the body is non-existent, being a projection into form of a non-existent thought. The split mind likewise is non-existent, but as long as we think we are separated, the thought of separation will be found in the mind. We think separation is here in the world, but this belief has no effect on the truth. For example, if we dream of Jesus while asleep, he is not in our dream, nor is he in our bedroom. He is a thought or symbol in the mind that we project into the dream. So, too, he is not in the world's dream of the body.

It is abundantly clear as you study his course that Jesus' only focus is purpose—*purpose is everything*. And so, again, what we made to hurt, the Holy Spirit uses to heal. This is the shift that characterizes the miracle. Once the form is made neutral, it can serve the ego's purpose of reinforcing guilt, separation, and the dream, or the Holy Spirit's purpose of undoing guilt through forgiveness and awakening us from the dream. Therefore, form is neither good nor bad; it just is. We made the world, and the only important thing now is which teacher we use to help us learn from it. To state it one last time, because of their prominent symbolism as instruments of guilt, abuse, power, pleasure, and pain, sex and money can be extraordinarily useful instruments to help us with undoing the ego and returning home. This passage from the workbook nicely summarizes the two purposes possible for the body—separate versus shared interests:

The body is a dream…. Made to be fearful, must the body serve the purpose given it. But we can change the purpose that the body will obey by changing what we think that it is for.

The body is the means by which God's Son returns to sanity. Though it was made to fence him into hell without escape, yet has the goal of Heaven been exchanged for the pursuit of hell. The Son of God extends his hand to reach his brother, and to help him walk along the road with him. Now is the body holy. Now it serves to heal the mind that it was made to kill (W-pII.5.3:1,4-5; 4).

* * * * * * * * * * *

Q: Are you saying that as you become more enlightened and your mind is healed, sex is not really required.

A: I am not saying or implying that at all. For certain, though, sex will stop being an issue, as will food, acquiring possessions, and anything else we think is so vital to us. Yet this does not mean that as we become more enlightened we are going to stop breathing, eating, drinking, or having sex. We may or we may not. These various physical activities may change in different ways, but their form is nothing. All that matters is that whatever we do, we do it with love instead of hate, peace instead of judgment.

Q: If you feel at times that you are lacking or struggling, the best solution for you is to ask to forgive, correct?

A: Correct. When you are having trouble, you need to recognize first that you are having trouble. Second, try to get past the temptation to attribute the cause of the unpleasantness or discomfort to something external. That attempt is the invitation to the Holy Spirit, and sets into motion the process of forgiveness. This means withdrawing the projection of blame from others, placing responsibility for your unhappiness within, then looking at the source of unhappiness you have chosen, realizing you chose it and so can choose again. The willingness to attribute the cause of your unhappiness to your mind's decision is the core of forgiveness, which you obviously cannot do with your ego. Even if you are not consciously thinking of the Holy Spirit or Jesus, you must have been asking Them for help; otherwise you would not have achieved that realization.

To repeat, realize you chose your situation. That is all you need know. You do not change your decision, which is the point of the statement: "The miracle establishes you dream a dream, and that its content is not true" (T-28.II.7:1). The passage says nothing about changing anything. The very fact that you are able to look at the wrong minded-thought system without judgment and guilt signals the end of the ego, for that is the choice for the Holy Spirit. This is the only change required, and what Jesus means by our needing only "a little willingness" (T-18.IV)—the willingness to look with him at the ego. This means you do not try to change it, for if you do, you but make its thought system real. Look, then, at your ego, but without judgment; look at the ways you have misused sex, money, and power, and their tremendous cost to you—but look without guilt. The ego has cost you the peace of God. Is anything here worth losing the experience of this peace, and the love that is just behind it?

5. Conclusion: From Form to Formlessness

I close with the last two paragraphs from Lesson 186, which nicely summarize how the Holy Spirit uses the forms of our lives to lead us to formlessness. What makes this process possible, as we have discussed, is the willingness to look at the forms—the behaviors—without guilt or judgment. This is what *A Course in Miracles* means by looking with the Holy Spirit or Jesus, and is all you need do. Simply look gently at how you have expressed the ego's thought system through separate interests. Realize but this— "of course this is what I would do"—and then see how the ego's thoughts of separation and guilt infuse the world you made.

It is essential that you look kindly at yourself and your ego's behaviors without accusation. You calmly acknowledge this is what you have done, and are therefore as insane as everyone else. But do realize you are insane, and that your decisions have inflicted tremendous pain on yourself. Set aside for the moment the pain they caused others, but be aware of how painful they have been for you. For this pain, that you no longer want, will motivate you to give up your misuse of the world as a way of reinforcing your special self, enabling you to turn to the Holy Spirit as your Friend, accept your special function, and be gently led through the forms of forgiveness to the Formlessness of God:

His gentle Voice is calling from the known to the unknowing. He would comfort you, although He knows no sorrow. He would make a restitution, though He is complete; a gift to you, although He knows that you have everything already. He has Thoughts which answer every need His Son perceives, although He sees them not. For Love must give, and what is given in His Name takes on the form most useful in a world of form.

These are the forms which never can deceive, because they come from Formlessness Itself. Forgiveness is an earthly form of love, which as it is in Heaven has no form. Yet what is needed here is given here as it is needed. In this form you can fulfill your function even here, although what love will mean to you when formlessness has been restored to you is greater still. Salvation of the world depends on you who can forgive. Such is your function here (W-pI.186.13-14).

APPENDIX

Question and Answer: Food

During a class held at the Foundation in 2005, a student related a conversation she had had with another Course student. They had been talking about foods that were thought to be healthful or not healthful. The following is an edited version of the dialogue between this student and Kenneth.

Q: Part of me knew that food was not the real issue, but on this level I thought that avoiding harmful food was reflecting a decision I made in my mind not to hurt myself. Then we began to talk about using microwave ovens. My friend said, "I know it's not going to hurt me because I'm using it in a loving way. I'm using it because I need to save myself time—it's convenient for me. But I still don't want to hurt myself. So the purpose is good." I am confused about this. On the one hand we can obviously be hurt by our choices, yet if our purpose is not to hurt ourselves, we could probably eat something that is potentially harmful and not be hurt.

A: This is an important issue. I have always said that students of *A Course in Miracles* ought to be normal. When they practice the Course they should use common sense. With regard to food, for example, we all have to eat. That is telling you that you are identified with your body, and that means at least a part of your mind identifies with the ego thought system. It is not helpful to deny that. As long as you identify with the ego and body, you will believe there are foods that are helpful and foods that are not—eating harmful foods is going to hurt you and eating healthful foods will benefit you, because that is what you believe. To deny that, as Jesus cautions us early in the text, is a "particularly unworthy form of denial" (T-2.IV.3:11). You obviously believe you are a body; therefore it is silly to then say "my thoughts are right, so it won't hurt me." If your thoughts were right, you would not be here, and you would not even address the issue; indeed, it would not even be an issue. So I think it is helpful to begin with the premise that your thoughts are not right. Therefore, you should eat the foods you believe will make you feel good, and avoid what you believe will make you feel bad. And then do not give it another thought. If you believe microwaving will radiate the food and have adverse effects on you, you should not use a microwave oven. And if you do not think it will do that, use it.

When you no longer are identified with a body, whether to use a microwave or not becomes a pseudo-issue. The whole thing is irrelevant. The only thing that is going to hurt you is guilt; the only thing that will help you is forgiveness. But very few people are

at that level. So while we are at the level of separation
—the body—do what you believe in. In other words,
it should not be an issue. It is a trap to think, "Well, if
I have loving thoughts while I use the microwave, the
loving thoughts will protect me"—as if the microwave can hurt you! You are already in an ego state of
mind when you find yourself believing that loving
thoughts can somehow affect something external.
That is the level confusion Jesus describes early in the
text (T-2.IV.2).

The mind, therefore, can have no real affect on the
body, for they are levels that have nothing to do with
each other. If I believe my loving thoughts will allow
me to eat genetically modified food without harm, I
am already harming myself, because I believe there is
a danger out there from which my loving thoughts can
protect me. I have thus committed the unforgivable
"sin" in this course: making the error real. This is no
different than beaming light to a troubled spot in the
world or to a troubled organ, or beaming loving
thoughts at a microwave. That is the mistake. The mistake is not in using or not using the microwave, but in
making it into an issue. I quoted Krishnamurti's line
before about sex: "Do it or don't do it, but get on with
it." Stop making it into a big deal. Microwaving is not
the issue; what the President of the United States de-
cides is not the issue; the world is not the issue. My

peace does not depend on an act of Congress, an act of the White House, or a microwave. My body might depend on that, and I certainly do not want to place my body in a vulnerable position as long as I think I am a body. But I also do not want to have the illusion that the world will make me safe. My only protection is forgiveness, because that alone will help me identify with love, our one safety.

Q: In the past you have given examples of people who had drug-induced experiences or healings, and you responded by saying it was really a reflection of their mind deciding to open up or be healed, and the experience reflected that decision; the drug was not really the cause. I thought that might be another part of the mistake I am making—that the wrong and right minds are reflected in our experiences. For instance, the world was made to attack or enjoy, but it is now neutral. It depends on the purpose that I am using it for. So, too, the body is now neutral. Can I apply that to a microwave?—that it was originally made to attack the body and God, but now is neutral, for the Holy Spirit can use everything for a different purpose.

A: As long as you think you are a body, you will judge some things in the world as harmful and others as helpful. As long as you do that—which is inevitable as a body—you better pay attention to the distinction.

Q: It seems like everything is really harmful—there is no limit.

A: Yes. We live in a world now where practically everything is harmful—the air we breathe, the water we drink, the food we eat, the bombs being dropped. This is a harmful world and it is important to see that, for it makes it unmistakably clear that we cannot trust anything outside. We can only go within, where true hope lies. Yet, once again, as long as we are in a body we should do what we feel is right. If we have ambivalence about a microwave, it would be silly to use it; there are other ways of heating up food. If time is extremely important for us, microwaving is wonderful, and so we should use it. In other words, we do the best we can, respect our preferences and belief systems, and act accordingly. Our focus should only be on not being harmful to ourselves or anyone else.

Another caution, try not to make microwaving into a spiritual lesson. That misses the point, and in doing so you are making the error real, a violation of the aforementioned cardinal principle of this course. As *The Song of Prayer* specifically states: "*Do not see error*. Do not make it real" (S-2.I.3:3-4). Agonizing over sex, money, a microwave, or anything else gives them a reality they do not have. That is the meaning of "Do it or don't do it, but get on with it." The form is never the issue. Once you get caught in the ego's trap—especially with food and health issues—it is hard not to be judgmental of people who do not agree with you, because you think what you are doing is so holy and spiritual. Yet there is nothing holy or spiritual about not microwaving. There is nothing holy or spiritual about microwaving. It is simply something a body does. Always begin with the basic premise that being in the body is an attack on God. It follows, then, that everything is an attack on God. So you do the best you can to forgive yourself.

Through your forgiveness, you learn to use the body positively, as a classroom that reflects back to you the mind's decision. If you find yourself agonizing over a microwave, for example, see that as a means of helping you realize that you are terrified of the love in your mind, and are displacing the internal conflict of love and your fear of it onto a microwave. What is helpful about that experience is that it is a red flag that says you had better look at this—this has nothing to do with the microwave, eating genetically modified foods, having meat or not having meat, or having a regular egg or an egg from a cage-free chicken. Do one or the other—whatever you feel is going to help you. But if it turns into a conflict, you know that you are displacing the conflict in your mind, because you are terrified of looking at it within and letting it go. At that point, however you resolve the problem outside is totally irrelevant.

110

Again, you should behave in whatever way works for you, but be sure to respect other people's doing the exact opposite. And one more thing, leave *A Course in Miracles* out of it. Do not bring it with you into a restaurant, a grocery store, your kitchen, or bedroom. This would be the worst thing you could do, because you would be making a situation into something real and special when it is not. The world is what it is—a simple projection of a thought of guilt. Undoing that thought should be your only focus. Therein lies your true peace and safety.

INDEX OF REFERENCES TO *A COURSE IN MIRACLES*

text

text (cont.)

text (cont.)

workbook for students

manual for teachers

Psychotherapy: Purpose, Process and Practice

Foundation for A Course in Miracles®

Kenneth Wapnick received his Ph.D. in Clinical Psychology in 1968 from Adelphi University. He was a close friend and associate of Helen Schucman and William Thetford, the two people whose joining together was the immediate stimulus for the scribing of A Course in Miracles. Kenneth had been involved with A Course in Miracles since 1973, writing, teaching, and integrating its principles with his practice of psychotherapy. He was on the Executive Board of the Foundation for Inner Peace, original publishers of A Course in Miracles.

Gloria Wapnick has a Master's degree in History from Hunter College (1970), and taught social studies in a New York City high school, where she was also Dean of Students. Gloria has been working with A Course in Miracles since 1977, and conducted her own group for several years.

In 1983 Kenneth and Gloria began the Foundation for A Course in Miracles, and in 1984 this evolved into a Teaching and Healing Center in Crompond, New York, which was quickly outgrown. In 1988 they opened the Academy and Retreat Center in upstate New York. In 1995 they began the Institute for Teaching Inner Peace through A Course in Miracles, an educational corporation chartered by the New York State Board of Regents. In 2001 the Foundation moved to Temecula, California and shifted its emphasis to electronic teaching. After Dr. Wapnick's death in 2013, it was decided to move to a smaller facility, which happened in October 2018 when the Foundation moved to Henderson, Nevada.

The following is Kenneth's and Gloria's vision of the Foundation:

In our early years of studying *A Course in Miracles,* as well as teaching and applying its principles in our respective professions of psychotherapy, and teaching and school administration, it seemed evident that this was not the simplest of thought systems to understand. This was so not only in the intellectual grasp of its teachings, but perhaps more importantly in the application of these teachings to our personal lives. Thus, it appeared to us from the beginning that the Course lent itself to teaching, parallel to the ongoing teachings of the Holy Spirit in the daily opportunities within our relationships which are discussed in the early pages of the manual for teachers.

One day several years ago while Helen Schucman and I (Kenneth) were discussing these ideas, she shared a vision that she had had of a teaching center as a white temple with a gold cross atop it. Although it was clear that this image was symbolic, we understood it to be representative of what the teaching center was to be: a place where the person of Jesus and his message in *A Course in Miracles* would be manifest. We have sometimes seen an image of a lighthouse shining its light into the sea, calling to it those passers-by who sought it. For us, this light is the

Course's teaching of forgiveness, which we would hope to share with those who are drawn to the Foundation's form of teaching and its vision of *A Course in Miracles*.

This vision entails the belief that Jesus gave the Course at this particular time in this particular form for several reasons. These include:

1) the necessity of healing the mind of its belief that attack is salvation; this is accomplished through forgiveness, the undoing of our belief in the reality of separation and guilt.

2) emphasizing the importance of Jesus and/or the Holy Spirit as our loving and gentle Teacher, and developing a personal relationship with this Teacher.

3) correcting the errors of Christianity, particularly where it has emphasized suffering, sacrifice, separation, and sacrament as being inherent in God's plan for salvation.

Our thinking has always been inspired by Plato (and his mentor Socrates), both the man and his teachings. Plato's Academy was a place where serious and thoughtful people came to study his philosophy in an atmosphere conducive to their learning, and then returned to their professions to implement what they were taught by the great philosopher. Thus, by integrating abstract philosophical ideals with experience, Plato's school seemed to be the perfect model for the teaching center that we directed for so many years.

We therefore see the Foundation's principal purpose as being to help students of *A Course in Miracles* deepen their understanding of its thought system, conceptually and experientially, so that they may be more effective instruments of Jesus' teaching in their own lives. Since teaching forgiveness without experiencing it is empty, one of the Foundation's specific goals is to help facilitate the process whereby people may be better able to know that their own sins are forgiven and that they are truly loved by God. Thus is the Holy Spirit able to extend His Love through them to others.

Related Material on *A Course in Miracles*

By Kenneth Wapnick, Ph.D.

Books, Downloadable ePUBS and PDFs
(www.facim.org)

Christian Psychology in *A Course in Miracles*.
Second edition, enlarged.
ISBN 978-0-933291-14-0 • #B-1 • Paperback • 94 pages
Audiobook • Read by Kenneth Wapnick (English)
ISBN 978-1-59142-593-9 • #AB-2 • one mp3 CD (2:10:31)
EPUB1dl • ISBN 978-1-59142-897-8

A Talk Given on *A Course in Miracles*: An Introduction.
Seventh edition.
ISBN 978-0-933291-16-4 • #B-3 • Paperback • 131 pages
EPUB3dl • ISBN 978-1-59142-575-5

Glossary-Index for *A Course in Miracles*.
Seventh edition, enlarged.
ISBN 978-0-933291-03-4 • #B-4 • Softcover • 247 pages
PDF4dl • ISBN 978-1-59142-908-1

Forgiveness and Jesus: The Meeting Place of *A Course in Miracles* and Christianity.
Seventh edition.
ISBN 978-0-933291-13-3 • #B-5 • Paperback • 330 pages
EPUB5dl • ISBN 978-1-59142-817-6

A Course in Miracles **and Christianity: A Dialogue.**
Second edition.
Kenneth Wapnick, Ph.D. and W. Norris Clarke, S.J.
ISBN 978-0-933291-18-8 • #B-13 • Paperback • 97 pages

The Most Commonly Asked Questions About *A Course in Miracles.* Second edition.
Gloria and Kenneth Wapnick, Ph.D.
ISBN 978-0-933291-21-8 • #B-14 • Paperback • 113 pages
EPUB14dl • ISBN 978-1-59142-621-9

The Message of *A Course in Miracles.*
Volume One: *All Are Called.*
Volume Two: *Few Choose to Listen.*
Volume One - 317 pages; Volume Two - 199 pages.
ISBN 978-0-933291-25-6 • #B-15 • Paperback (two-volume set)
EPUB15dl • ISBN 978-1-59142-622-6

The Journey Home: "The Obstacles to Peace" in
A Course in Miracles.
ISBN 978-0-933291-24-9 • #B-16 • paperback • 511 pages
EPUB16dl • ISBN 978-1-59142-901-2

Ending Our Resistance to Love: The Practice of
A Course in Miracles.
ISBN 978-1-59142-132-0 • #B-17 • paperback • 94 pages
Audiobook • Read by Loral Reeves (English)
ISBN 978-1-59142-364-5 • #AB-17 • one mp3 CD (2:25:34)
EPUB17dl • ISBN 978-1-59142-568-7

Life, Death, and Love: Shakespeare's Great Tragedies and *A Course in Miracles*. Volume One: *King Lear* • "Love and Be Silent": Forgiveness and Defenselessness. Volume Two: *Hamlet* • "To Be or Not to Be": Death Leaves Not Its Source. Volume Three: *Macbeth* • "A Tale Told by an Idiot": The Murderous World of Guilt. Volume Four: *Othello* • "Loving Not Wisely but Too Well": The Tragedy of Specialness.

Volume One - 106 pages; Volume Two - 104 pages; Volume Three - 82 pages; Volume Four - 91 pages.
ISBN-13 978-1-59142-142-9 • #B-18 • Paperback (four-volume boxed set)
EPUB13dl • ISBN 978-1-59142-747-6

The Healing Power of Kindness. Volume One: Releasing Judgment. Second edition.
ISBN 978-1-59142-147-4 • #B19 • Paperback • 119 pages
Audiobook • Read by Loral Reeves (English)
ISBN 978-1-59142-459-8 • #AB-19 • one mp3 CD (2:57:07)
EPUB19dl • ISBN 978-1-59142-569-4

The Healing Power of Kindness. Volume Two: Forgiving Our Limitations.
ISBN 978-1-59142-155-9 • #B-20 • Paperback • 118 pages
EPUB20dl • ISBN 978-1-59142-570-0

Form versus Content: Sex and Money.
ISBN 978-1-59142-194-8 • #B-21 • Paperback • 116 pages
EPUB21dl • ISBN 978-1-59142-755-1

Parents and Children: Our Most Difficult Classroom.
Two-volume set: Part 1 - 126 pages; Part 2 - 89 pages
ISBN 978-1-59142-205-1 • #B-22 • Paperback (two-volume set)
EPUB22dl • ISBN 978-1-59142-576-2

Journey through the Workbook of *A Course in Miracles*. Commentary on the 365 Lessons.
Volume One - 195 pages; Volume Two - 121 pages; Volume Three - 111 pages; Volume Four - 186 pages; Volume Five - 163 pages; Volume Six - 160 pages; Volume Seven -220 pages; Volume Eight (Index/Appendix) - 68 pages
ISBN 978-1-59142-206-8 • #B-23 • Paperback (eight-volume boxed set) 1,224 pages
EPUB23dl • ISBN 978-1-59142-767-4

Journey through the Manual of *A Course in Miracles*.
ISBN 978-1-59142-207-5 • #B-24 • Paperback (one-volume boxed set) • 246 pages
EPUB24dl • To be released 2018

"What It Says": From the Preface of *A Course in Miracles*.
ISBN 978-1-59142-208-2 • #B-25 • Paperback • 78 pages
EPUB25dl • ISBN 978-1-59142-756-8

From Futility to Happiness: Sisyphus as Everyman.
ISBN 978-1-59142-209-9 • #B-26 • Paperback • 145 pages
EPUB26dl • ISBN 978-1-59142-571-7

The Arch of Forgiveness.
ISBN 978-1-59142-210-5 • #B-27 • Paperback • 103 pages
EPUB27dl • ISBN 978-1-59142-577-9

The Stages of Our Spiritual Journey.
ISBN 978-1-59142-441-3 • #B-28 • Paperback • 161 pages
EPUB28dl • ISBN 978-1-59142-572-4

Ending Our Escape from Love: From Dissociation to Acceptance of *A Course in Miracles*.
ISBN 978-1-59142-513-7 • #B-29 • Paperback • 143 pages
EPUB29dl • ISBN 978-1-59142-573-1

Healing the Unhealed Mind.
ISBN 978-1-59142-546-5 • #B-30 • Paperback • 144 pages
EPUB30dl • ISBN 978-1-59142-574-8

When 2 + 2 = 5: Reflecting Love in a Loveless World.
ISBN 978-1-59142-578-6 • #B-31 • Paperback • 173 pages
EPUB31dl • ISBN 978-1-59142-589-2

Journey through the Text of *A Course in Miracles*.
ISBN 978-1-59142-748-3 • #B-32 • Paperback 1,146 pages
(sold only as four volume set)
EPUB32dl • ISBN 978-1-59142-869-5

Taking the Ego Lightly: Protecting Our Projections.
ISBN 978-1-59142-749-0 • #B-33 • Paperback • 98 pages
EPUB33dl • ISBN 978-1-59142-752-0

From The Lighthouse: An Anthology. To Look Upon Darkness Through Light Must Dispel It.
ISBN 978-1-59142-827-5 • #B-34 • Hardcover • 520 pages

From The Lighthouse: An Anthology. To Look Upon
Darkness Through Light Must Dispel It. Volume One.
EPUB34-1dl • ISBN: 978-1-59142-764-3

From The Lighthouse: An Anthology. To Look Upon
Darkness Through Light Must Dispel It. Volume Two.
EPUB34-2dl • ISBN: 978-1-59142-765-0

From The Lighthouse: An Anthology. To Look Upon
Darkness Through Light Must Dispel It. Volume Three.
EPUB34-3dl • ISBN: 978-1-59142-766-7

**A Symphony of Love. Selections of Dr Kenneth
Wapnick's Writings: Autobiographies, Poetry, Short
Stories, and Articles.**
Edited by Gloria Wapnick
ISBN 978-1-59142-876-3 • #B-35 • Paperback • 484 pages
PDF35dl • ISBN 978-1-59142-910-4

**Q&A: Detailed Answers to Student-Generated
Questions on the Theory and Practice of *A Course in
Miracles*.**
Supervised and Edited by Kenneth Wapnick, Ph.D.
PDF36dl • 1,284 pages

Made in the USA
Monee, IL
09 October 2021